The Wild Feminine

Stories to Inspire and Enbolden

By Marilyn Steele, Ph.D.

ISBN: 978-1482386066

The Wild Feminine

www.thewildfeminine.com

Dedication

To my amazing, loving, and supportive children. Jeremy, for his courage, sense of humor, and help with tasks large and small. Susannah, for her radiant spirit, creative brilliance and generous encouragement. Azzia, for her exceptional technological wizardry, design gifts, patience and perseverance in helping to birth this book.

To their beloveds, Monica, Michael, and Nick, and a tribe of cherished grandchildren: Marina, Carlo, Welden, Jeb, Brody, River, and those on the way.

May their future, and the future of all the world's children, be abundant in love and peace.

Earlier versions of some chapters in this book were previously published.

Default in *Left Curve*

Herstory in *Griffin*

Life in the Round in *Lalitamba*

Shooting Star: A Letter to Janet in *Psychological Perspectives*

Singing in Tree in *SageWoman* and *Zone 3*

Uncharted Waters in *Down Dirty Word*

Table of Contents

Introduction

Growing up in Hawaii, I was rooted in the beauties of a wild place, surrounded by an indigenous culture where the Feminine and the land were sacred. We told ghost stories around the campfire about Pele, goddess of fire, whose passion and creativity created new lands. I spent most of my time outside, immersed in the rhythms of the ocean, the soothing scents, sounds and spirits of the island. Books and animals were my steady companions.

Many of the stories in this book take place in nature, describing my awe, wonder, joy in the endless diversity of wondrous living things. There are miracles in these stories, and hard lessons I learned about right timing, which often did not follow my own plans. There are many paths I took in search of intellectual knowledge and spiritual truths to answer my questions about who I am, why I am here, what am I for. Along the way, many dreams, visions and synchronicities came to find me.

As a single mother of two in my thirties, I entered graduate school with these burning questions: What does a healthy woman look like? Where are her stories, in her own voice? What about Herstory? I could not find myself or ways to understand my journey in the psychological models that diminished women, made them secondary and inferior to male attributes and development. I was determined to find new models, a new pattern, which could describe the unfolding of women's lives, a description that includes at its core a woman's soul.

To do this, I had to learn a new way of seeing and discovering the pattern that connects. In my research, I chose women who defined themselves as artists regardless of their age or relationships status. I was fascinated by how their lives had unfolded, how change, transformation, growth occurred. Without exception, there were periods of turbulence and chaos followed by a total shift in consciousness, a changed life. The truth began to emerge that spirituality and science, Jungian psychology and the creative process, are all in correspondence.

The stories in this book weave three levels of experience: First, my individual, personal experiences. Second, the patriarchal cultural context of shared values and assumptions. And third, the deepest layers of the archetypal collective unconscious where dreams, intuition, myths, synchronicities, strange attractors live and show us other worlds of meaning.

You, dear reader, may be aware of a feeling of great change, that time is speeding up. There is an intensity, an unsettled state. This is good news. In this chaos, this overflowing wealth of possibilities, we participate with our attention, our beliefs, our intention and the actions that arise from those to create our future.

We carry the vision of the emerging possible.

Although we cannot make synchronicities or numinous experiences happen, there is much we can do to prepare ourselves. In every moment there are possibilities for us to hope, believe and act upon the mysteries of an unfolding universe. We can learn to use our intuition, to listen for the still, small voice within, to notice what is happening around us, to honor our energy, which informs us of our deepest truths. Thus we are carried forward into wholeness and holiness.

My purpose and goal for this book is to inspire and embolden women to emerge, arise, spring out into their full power and use their wisdom to change the world.

One of the languages of the soul is poetry. So although I included a Resources section at the end of the book, there are no poetry anthologies listed. There are just too many wonderful poems. Read many, any, and often.

What a blessing to be in this time, and not alone in the task to bring feminine power and wisdom back to the world. I celebrate and honor each of you, devoted to being your truest and biggest selves, offering your hands and heart, mind and soul, to the vision of a more peaceful and loving world. These stories and essays are my offering. May they enliven the Wild Feminine in you.

Default

"Change is possible with a wild heart."

- Terry Tempest Williams

Clicking my new dove-gray Joan & David heels on the marble floor, I show up at the Alameda County Courthouse in Hayward to appear before the Superior Court of California for the third time. It is September 2009. In my brand-new three-piece Tahari suit, pink and gray, I carry a honey-brown Italian briefcase filled with the records, weapons of truth, regarding my default case. The briefcase is not well-coordinated with the rest of my armor, but holds its own with the black briefcases of the many attorneys filing through the metal detectors and conveyor belt where we place our accessories in the little blue boxes. I almost look like one of the lawyers and walk briskly past the lines of traffic offenders and families with small children and a hundred sad stories. When I get to the court door, it is locked. The lawyer who represented Capital One at the first hearing is sitting down. I stand in my excruciating but gorgeous high heels and turn my back to her. I am steeling myself for this next appearance, for the speech I am going to give to the judge, for all the tens of thousands of citizens I know are hounded by credit card banks with their criminal rates of interest, fees, fines, and so many other predatory practices. I will stand for the rule of law, for democracy, for the rights of the little people.

A deputy opens the heavy wooden court door, and we file in. There is no judge. The clerk announces that she is out sick. The lawyers are muttering about their cases being postponed. My stomach lurches. I don't think I can do this again. As I sit straight-spined, attempting to be brave, the attorney from the last court date, on behalf of Capital One, approaches me.

"I'm not here on that case, and the other lawyer they sometimes call isn't here for them either. I don't think they sent anybody."

When the clerk calls me to the front of the

courtroom, no one stands for the other side. I start to relax.

"The judge will want to see you in two months."

"Can't you just dismiss it? They didn't have representation last time either."

She laughs. "I'm just the clerk!" She wants to wait to see if anybody shows up or calls in. I take my seat again. The previous opposing lawyer, Wendy, winks and whispers, "Good luck" as she leaves.

As I sit waiting, praying that no one will show up for Capital One, I replay the long approach to this moment. My youngest child's long illness. My own cancer diagnosis in 2001, early stage endometrial cancer. Grateful to have insurance and an early diagnosis, it was a shock to find out after surgery and an uncomplicated four-day hospital stay that $17,000 of the medical expenses were not covered. Blue Cross was disputing their share of a $44,000 bill. It took a year to fight for those benefits, repeatedly sending copies of forms they "lost," addressing charges of getting insurance falsely with a preexisting condition. Then they raised my premiums so high that I could no longer afford insurance.

In 2002, I tried to start an educational seminar business to compensate for a flagging psychotherapy practice. The brochures, mailing costs, and room rentals also went on my credit cards. Rewarding as the seminars were, I lost money. Drowning in debt, staggering under the 29% credit card interest rates, I closed all credit card accounts in the summer of 2004 after trying first to negotiate lower interest or deferrals of payment.

I never imagined this small Capital One account, $2,200 when it closed, would become $5,231.65 declared in "A Request for Entry of Default" and more tortuous to resolve than the other three larger accounts I had settled with Wells Fargo, Discover Card, and Household Finance. But after several different collection agencies, this Capital One account was acquired by the law firm of Brachfeld and Associates. Although they had refused my first settlement offer of $1,250 in the summer of 2007, I was confident that we could negotiate eventually. Meanwhile, I would make regular and automatic withdrawal payments of $100. Plus $7.50 for "processing." My contact person in Texas, Marge, assured me that our payment agreement would keep the claim out of court. But one afternoon in February 2008, a knock on my front door turned out to be a summons server. Furious, I called Marge.

"We had a deal! What is this court summons about?"

"Oh, don't worry, dear, that has nothing to do with

our deal. It doesn't mean a thing."

I knew better.

In 2007, while I was attempting to handle a court summons from Discover Card by mistakenly making arrangements with the pirates at Gerald Moore and Company, they slipped by a default judgment for over $7,000 and froze both my checking and savings accounts. I could not touch any of my money without dealing with the county sheriff. Getting default judgments from unaware or overwhelmed or terrified people happens all the time. I was advised by the lawyer friend of a friend that I would have to pay the judgment. That was just not right, even if it was "legal."

I began keeping income from my therapy practice in cash and set up a new bank account in another county. At the sheriff's office, on Good Friday, I arrived with my tax papers, bank statement, and a trembling thimbleful of courage as I stood in this room of merry bondsmen holding piles of filings and summons. The stern woman at the window stared at me over her glasses. I asked if I could file these papers, please. Silent for a moment as she looked at my file, she glanced at her computer. Announced:

"That lien has been terminated."

"It what?"

"That lien has been terminated."

"Does that mean…gone?" There were a few laughs in the room. She showed the hint of a smile.

"Yes."

"What happened?"

"It was not filed in a timely manner."

"Oh my god, an Easter miracle!" I cried. "And you are an angel!"

Not quite done, after I settled my Discover Card account I received a threatening letter from a new debt collection law firm regarding the same settled claim. With the letter was a legal form titled "Substitution of Attorney-Civil" signed by an attorney, Dominic Delfin. Assuming at first an honest mistake in data and record keeping, I immediately called to correct their records. The agent in the legal department listened for a moment.

Then he sneered, "Oh yeah? Can you prove it?"

The heat rose up my spine, bursting into flame out the top of my head.

"Yes, I can prove it, you asshole!"

"There is no need for that language," he said. "I'm here to service your loan." There's another word for that service.

For the next hour, I frantically went through the

financial drawer, the check statement drawer, and the scary debt collection files in search of the letter I know I had gotten verifying settlement in full after months of telephone negotiations. I also remembered after a year had passed having a ceremony to burn the most painful files and memories, the fat Discover Card file that showed five years of personal life mess flooding into debt. It felt toxic to have the file still in my house, in my life. But I would have kept that most important paper, wouldn't I? Of course. And if I hadn't, I could retrace my steps through the bank, the check I wrote.

Exhausted, I opened the financial drawer in the sideboard one last time. The lovely antique sideboard that in another life, in my previous life, would have held linens for entertaining, beautiful napkins and napkin holders, place mats, seasonal centerpieces. Instead, it was crammed with financial records, spending and earning for four years. Taking a last look, I found a thin folder with the remaining three pieces of paper from the original file. The letter of proof was there.

I checked with the state bar to see if this suspicious "Dominic Delfin" lawyer was legitimate. No such lawyer licensed to practice in the state. I researched all of the federal and state laws I could find on Google. Especially egregious under the Fair Debt Collection Practices Act was the deceptive representation of an attorney in an effort to intimidate me. I cited this and California State Law regarding deceptive forms in my response and mentioned that I was considering filing a civil suit. My little credit card loans were bundled and passed along like a hot potato, no one wanting to interrupt the line until they had gotten their share.

So this year, when I hung up with Marge, I knew what to do about a summons. It was not to keep talking to the collection agency pirates. I immediately filed a response with the court disputing the amount and sped across town to change my checking account with the automatic withdrawal arrangement. But not before they took another unauthorized $107.50. Then I went to the Berkeley Law Clinic, another collection of angels, three of whom would help me win this Capital One case. And did some research.

Elizabeth Warren, who oversaw the federal bailout oversight team and is now a Senator, helped me enormously through her books on the credit card industry. I learned that in 2005, nearly half of all US bankruptcies were filed by working families in the aftermath of a major illness or injury, even though three out of four had health insurance at the time. In 2007, the fastest-growing group to declare bankruptcy was those 55 and older, nearly one in four declarers. Is this any way to treat our elders? I wonder what kind of country we would have if it had begun with the "Founding Mothers." Or had our Constitution, modeled on the Iroquois Confederacy, not excluded the essential Council of Clan Mothers, wise and powerful Grandmothers who determined the priorities for the Confederacy, especially whether or not to go to war. As author Michael Lewis said about 2008: "One of the distinctive traits of the financial disaster was…how little women had to do with it."

We continue to be the largest arms dealer in the world and the country with the most guns per capita. Right up there with Yemen. Many of the customers for US weapons are in the developing world and are repressive, undemocratic regimes, thus fueling more violence and instability. We spend almost 50% of our budget on "defense," on the military, which in 2006 was almost as much as the rest of the world spent, combined. The building of prisons is apparently more important than the building of bridges, of schools. One in five American children is hungry. We are the only Western industrialized country that does not provide universal health care. We have an abysmal rate of infant mortality and one in five children living in poverty. Speed and greed. The laser focus, the linear timeline, denying the fundamental scientific and spiritual truth of our interdependence and defaulting on the promises of democracy. This is a deeply systemic illness. A moral crisis. A soul sickness. This culture of corruption and greed, the chilling absence of an ethic of care. It is time to reimagine what real wealth is and what kind of a country we want to be. We can no longer pretend to be a free market. Profits do not trickle down.

Money has been confused with wealth.

If women were in charge, if the principles of the sacred feminine—care, connection, creativity—were valued, what would our society, our world, our planet look like?

Now, as I continue to sit in the courtroom, I decide to pray, to visualize; maybe a little new consciousness will help. Closing my eyes, I place my hands in front of my belly, a few inches apart, and picture a white heat expanding. *Let there be peace around this issue.* The clerk calls my name to schedule the next hearing. As she looks at the computer screen, she exclaims:

"Oh! This case was dismissed yesterday!"

"You're kidding."

"Nope."

"Could I have that in writing?"

There are a few chuckles. I do not take the opportunity to speak out for democracy, being so relieved that I can leave as a free woman. There will be plenty of time for that in the years to come.

Moonstone, Touchstone

Early this morning, I woke up to a full moon resting on the steeple of the tall redwood tree I call Grandmother. The sky was still cloudy, veiled by rain and snow and hail hiding all the mysteries of life not yet formed. Just beneath the grays and whites, extending straight out from the tree arms, a long ribbon of lavender. A feeling of wonder still remains from last night, when it snowed here in the Berkeley hills. First, I watched the raccoon families file in to eat, shoulder to shoulder at the food bowls with feral cat Chiaroscuro and the skunk I call Lily, her exuberant tail in full blossom. Then the snow began to fall, sending our extended family loping and skipping and slinking into the dark.

Now as I gaze skyward at the gold glowing circle, I think of the Grandmothers in a dream who brought the moon to me long ago. First, the very old thin woman walking with a cane showed me the bridge to another world, lit by a moon so huge it filled the sky. It floated close enough to touch. A silken, luminous lemon yellow, rose pink and silver white like a shimmering abalone shell. Ten years later I dreamed of a Jung Institute dinner with analysts and candidates. An elegant silver haired woman was going around the oval table, giving gifts to each person, a symbol of our own gifts, our way of being and traveling in the world. When she got to me, I said something about needing to take care of my children. She laughed and reminded me I was old enough to have grandchildren and it was time to do my work in the world. She put a moonstone into my hands and said: "This is your work." Don Sandner, Jungian analyst and shaman, smiled when I told him. And said: "Of course. Jung's psychology is a moon psychology, not solar like Freud's, and yours is a lunar consciousness."

The moon is the gateway between heaven and earth, the threshold between earthly ego and transcendent

Self. It symbolizes the diffuse, integrated and textured consciousness of the Feminine. This mode of awareness connects us to cycles of waxing and waning, to the darkness of the night, to the life rhythms of life, death and rebirth. Women's egos function in a similar fashion, receiving transpersonal images and energies from the collective unconscious. There are ways to strengthen this native capacity.

Psychologically, the feminine principle is the portal or gateway between the personal and the transpersonal. The role of the female shaman is that of midwife for passages. Our powers come from the moon, and in our bodies we unite both our spiritual and material beings. Giver of dreams, omens, revelations, the moon governs the movement of the tides. It symbolizes the principle of transformation, moving in its own cycles of waxing and waning, of darkening and disappearing.

We learn from the moon how to follow our own rising and falling rhythms of energies, of feelings. We learn to listen for the inner voice, the voice of the oracle that has secrets to tell.

The lunar spirit is connected to time, to actual, embodied life. The particular. The concrete. The unique. It is not an abstract and disembodied concept. It is related to the earth, to the heart, as the moon is the gateway between heaven and earth, integrating our spiritual and physical being. Using a lunar consciousness, we attend to a time being favorable or unfavorable, depending on whether spiritual energy turns toward the ego and reveals itself or turns away, darkens and disappears or ripens. There are times for watching, waiting, placing oneself in harmony with the timing of our soul's purposes. Women in tune with this consciousness move with the transformative power that brings in the tides. It is always concerned with wholeness, with shaping and realizing. With creating and manifesting. Such a woman perceives what is hidden, veiled, mysterious.

Processes of growth are also transformations of the self. They require periods of darkness and invisibility, of stillness and quiet. They ask of us faith, patience. An acceptance of carrying the questions until the knowledge is ripe and ready for the light of day. We muse, ponder, contemplate, circumambulate until the true meaning arises. We learn to watch for signs, for the right relationship to the situation, to moving with the waxing and waning of doubts and uncertainties. The mysteries of moon knowledge require valuing the intuitive, the instinctual. It is more like a ripening, a conception, waiting for things to surface and come into consciousness. Learning to keep still until the fruit of the moon tree, the tree of life, has ripened into fullness can be difficult. To carry a knowledge and allow it to ripen. This is not a passive activity, however. Unlike the feminine symbols of the cup, chalice, and grail, the moon refers to the generative, transformative aspects of the feminine, the cyclical and dynamic aspects of change and transformation.

The seat of matriarchal consciousness is not in the head but in the heart. In order to shine forth, as in creative work, all feelings need to be included. Originally, in the first creation story, the sun and the moon were created as equal in power and value. Then Adam's first wife, Lilith, was replaced by Eve, and the power of the feminine was denigrated and diminished, a process that continues in Western culture today.

We tend, especially in the United States, to value only the unremitting focus and constant speeded up activity of a solar or masculine consciousness. In this concentrated glaring heat, narrow focus and speed, much is scorched and carelessly destroyed.

This feminine consciousness is also closely related to music, dance, and rhythm. It is closely related to shamanism, to prophecy, to the conception of new life and new possibility. This requires openness, receptivity, and a willingness to accept and receive emerging content and come into harmony with it.

Matriarchal consciousness exists in all human beings, but women are closer to it, native to it. Only a matriarchal consciousness can recognize the individual time element. It is a particular, singular, concrete and grounded sense of time that is contextual, relational. This is not a passive task.

> They wished to flower
> and flowering is being beautiful
> but we wish to ripen
> and that means being dark and taking pains.
> - Rilke

We learn about spiritual renewal from the moon, which always returns after three days of darkness.

Lunar consciousness is of the ego, it is not unconscious. But it is more inclusive and embodied than a narrow, sterile intellect. Although it may move in a different rhythm than the speed of the solar masculine, this is not due to incapacity for action. Instead, it requires a willingness to surrender to the mysteries of life and a greater wisdom of alignment with the deeper laws of nature, of Spirit.

The moment of conception is veiled and mysterious. The knowledge revealed is the same kind as that imparted in the true mysteries. It consists not of truths imparted from the outside but of experienced inner transformations. The seat of matriarchal consciousness is in the heart, and includes what has meaning and value. This is the source of creativity.

From etymology, we learn these aspects of the word moon from the original Sanskrit. Our feminine qualities are rooted here, too:

Menos, spirit heart soul, courage. *Menoinan,* to consider, meditate, wish. Also *manteia*, prophecy, *memini*, to remember, and from the Sanskrit: *mati-h*, thought, knowing. Dreaming, *metiesthai*, and *metis*, wisdom, come from the moon and belong to women and the feminine.

> "The stone which the builders rejected has become the cornerstone."
>
> - Psalm 118:22

As we have moved into the Age of Aquarius, a

massive wave of creativity has become visible. This emergence is being carried by the returning Feminine archetype that offers a new foundation for personal and planetary healing.

The Iroquois believed that dreams expressed the secret desires of the soul. It was a sacred duty to help dreamers read the language of the soul and take appropriate action. In dreams our eyes are opened. We awaken to the messages of our Higher Self. A dream is a journey. It matters. And the powers of the Dreaming are closely connected to the land. Indigenous dreamers not only listen to the earth, they also speak for it and seek to sustain the web of connection between humans and the cosmos.

Our dreams may lead us into what the Aborigines call the Dreamtime, which is creation time. It not only tells us about the origin of things but it is right now the seedbed of the many dimensions of life. In the Dreaming we may be able to see and know new possibilities, ways for soul retrieval for our culture, the healing of all our relations.

To find the shaman within, we do not have to travel to exotic foreign countries or hunt assiduously through the vestiges of the past. We can experience directly the sacred universe without intermediary. Shamanism is deeply rooted in the body, in our dreams, in the myths that live in the archetypal layers of our being and in our connection to nature. We all dream, every single night, whether or not we remember. We women are wisdom-keepers. We all have the capacity and cellular memory for experiencing both our sacred and material natures. This capacity can be cultivated, strengthened, so that we may know the joys, the magic, the power of living in both worlds. In these ways we live our larger stories, maintaining a fruitful relationship between ego and Self, soul. There are ways to welcome the shaman within, the dream maker, the magic manifestor. Renewal and soul retrieval can be found right here. In the present moment. In your everyday life.

There is a practice in shamanism called deep listening. An indigenous elder called it "listening with the skin." The answers lie in nature, and also in our own inner wisdom. We must move the energy and our thinking from our heads to our hearts. As Sandra Ingerman says, "We must remember what we love about life and what brings us to a place of awe and wonder, reigniting our passion."

One of the shamanic traditions is the way of the Adventurer rather than the Warrior. Although the Adventurer acknowledges there are dangers in the world, she experiences the world as an exciting place full of opportunity to make it what you will. She seeks power not only for herself but to create and change experience and to help others to do the same. She uses the power of belief. As the Warrior is alert to dangers, the Adventurer is aware of connections. It is well represented and taught in the Hawaiian teachings of Huna, where the focus is on enjoyment, love, and creating peace in the community. The shaman in all traditions practices the accumulation of inner power.

Living close to the heart of the Divine is not about becoming holy or elevated or perfect. It is the process of becoming more fully and deeply human. Here's a story about that from a Sufi master:

One day a man from Mount Locam came to visit Sari al-Saqati.

'Sheikh So-and-So from Mount Locam greets you,' he said.

'He dwells in the mountains,' commented Sari. 'So his efforts amount to nothing. A man ought to be able to live in the midst of the market and be so preoccupied with God that not for a single minute is he absent from God.'

- Sari in *Traveling the Path of Love*

The moon reminds us that our fullness and our power comes from the circle.

Lame Deer, Lakota Sioux medicine man says:

"You have noticed that everything an Indian does is in a circle, and that is because the Power of the world always works in circles, and everything tries to be round... The sky is round, and I have heard that the earth is round like a ball and so are all the stars. The wind in its greatest power, whirls. Birds make their nests in circles, for theirs is the same religion as ours. The sun comes forth and goes down again in a circle. The moon does the same, and both are round. Even the seasons form a great circle in their changing, and always come back again to where they were."

Women's leadership most effectively functions in the round, with a network, web, lattice of relationships, shared information and inspiration.

Last night I dreamed:

I stand with other women in the countryside at the bottom of a grassy hill, the full moon above us. We wear flowered scarves over our heads, long swirling skirts, waiting for some honored person. The crowd gasps as she arrives. A six foot tall woman strides down the hill with a cauldron on her head, fire burning in her eyes. Her skirt is flung out from her slim hips by the speed and power of her walking. She passes by so close to me I could almost touch her. She fixes me with her blazing eyes. The crowd murmurs "It is Astarte."

Syrian Astarte. Goddess of Enlightenment. Queen of the Stars, the moon. Perhaps she is drawing near.

"Another world is not only possible, she is on her way. On a quiet day, I can hear her breathing."

- Arundhati Roy

Angels and Skunks

I'm sitting in the backyard, wilderness that it is, relaxing. There is a slight lingering scent of the skunk family that visited last night. A mother and her six little babies, barely visible under their unfurled tails. They spread out to frolic, to look for food, twirling in circles as if on wheels. When they had roamed for enough time, mom gave a whistle, a squeak, and they glided so close that only her huge tail was visible and they moved off as one great black and white fur cascade.

It's too hot to do anything today like think, worry, or even read *People*. I decided to just sit here because it is a beautiful day, the sky is robin's egg blue, these wonderful self sufficient trees are new spring green, and because it is finally sinking in five years later: this is my home. This is my yard. I get to keep it. And I don't have to keep fighting for it. It's a gift. Another miracle.

Five years ago, buying this house looked totally impossible. The real estate market was insanely hot, with multiple bids over the asking prices - $400,000 for a cottage in the flatlands, and here in the hills with a view of the reddish orange Golden Gate Bridge I didn't have a prayer. In 1998 I had exactly two weeks to find a legal Berkeley address.

We were leaving for Italy, a trip for the family, to introduce the kids to beautiful Florence and show them where I'd gone to school thirty years before. High school would begin right after our return.

Azzia had been disenrolled from Berkeley High when they found out I had lied about my Emeryville residence, using my office address to get her into this school district. Embarrassed but undaunted, I found this cottage listed for rent, loving it after just a five minute viewing from outside. I followed the owner everywhere, bringing him lattes, dressing in my business finery, making no extra demands. He agreed to sign the two-year lease before holding an open house, anxious to get back to New York. At the time I took all the credit for being assertive, effective, smart and charming. I later had to amend that perception when I could not get the landlord to attend to the mushrooms growing on the inside of the front door, the rusted water heater that was leaking water, or the awnings across the front picture windows which had flapped and frayed away to tatters. Apparently my most winning attribute was being so nice they thought I would be No Trouble.

When they announced in a formal letter (wife is a real estate lawyer) one year later that they were going to sell and wanted me out, I was furious and terrified, but being the Mom meant I needed to deal with it in some hopeful, mature, fierce way.

In Berkeley even renting was impossible. A two-bedroom apartment on the third floor downtown was $2000 a month, to the $1600 I was paying for rent. No yard, no raccoons, no deer, no trees. No sanity, no soul. Was it time to move out of the Bay Area? Then where? Colorado? Hawaii? How to choose where you belong? Surely not by the cost of the rent or mortgage. At some point I took a deep breath, and I remembered the two year part of the lease. I said "No, we're staying, and I want to buy it." More jousting letters were exchanged. What a burst of bravado. Bluff. I would use the year to find some way to do this.

Living in the house was a great advantage. I scheduled a report from a structural engineer, hoping for bad news, and an inspection from a building contractor, Bert Graystone. He called a couple of weeks later to say there was a tricky situation: He had been recommended to the owners for their own inspection. What a perfect proof of legitimacy! I pleaded with him. Mercifully he agreed to keep working for me, and would do what he could to help. Not that the report was dishonest. It just estimated on the high side of all the necessary repairs. I was busy trying to find money for a down payment and hide my anxiety from Azzia; my resources short by a few tens of thousands. My parents - bless them - gave me $20,000. Partly they felt bad because they had broken a promise two years before to help with a house purchase only to pull their money out when we opened escrow. That was pretty bad. I asked other relatives for loans, my truly rich uncle who said this was a bad investment, my sister whose billionaire husband owns three houses, including a historical mansion. That request, along with my business plan, tax returns, plan for repayment was back on my doorstep 24 hours later in a bright red Fed Ex envelope. "Good luck to you, a loan would be awkward." Thank God that didn't work, but at the time it left me desperate.

Defeated, heartsick, I crawled out of bed the Thursday before Open House Sunday, the day all the real estate brokers come to stake their claims. I couldn't bear being in the house while they put numbers to pieces of my heartspace. The owner's broker was pounding a "For Sale" sign next to the driveway. Why not just put that stake into my heart? I said with my glaring eyes, while I smiled politely. A drawing of the house included a promise for expanding potential, space to build an addition on the hill.

Which explained why the work crew had done a scorched earth clearing of the, my, backyard the previous week.

When I got back Thursday night, no one had been inside. The broker had the wrong key, and fourteen visiting agents had to turn around and go home.

The next day, my neighbor, a woman in her fifties with curly brown hair and large horn rimmed glasses whose name I didn't know, came by to find out what was happening. We sat here on the patio, next to the desert wasteland , Kori and I. She told me how much she and her husband liked having Azzia and me as neighbors. We seemed nice, quiet, she admired single mothers, and we didn't have a dog. Also, she and her husband didn't want anyone building on the hill. I told her how much we loved living here, all the ways I had tried to find more money that hadn't worked out, the rejected first and only bid I had in me, and the looming dread of Open House Sunday mob day.

"How much more money do you think you need? Would $60,000 help?"

I looked into the eyes of this stranger, this angel, and everything got very, very quiet while the world rearranged itself. I turned from the familiarity of my old family into a new mystery. Is this the Twilight Zone? Is she crazy? Does her husband know she's over here? I stalled.

"Well, why don't you talk to - what's your husband's name?"

"Steve."

"Steve. And let's talk tomorrow."

The next day, more steady, I responded: "I don't think I need $60,000 but $40,000 might work."

On Saturday we made an agreement for a $40,000 loan, and I faxed the new offer to the owners. They wanted to wait for the Open House, expected a bidding war. Early

Sunday morning Kori came over to keep me company. There were three early birds who arrived before the official starting time, and I met them at the front door in my friendly hostess guise. To the first - a lean, bearded, olive skinned man - I said indeed there were things I liked about living here as a renter for two years: the view of course is spectacular (as we turned to admire it together) but there were just a few little things that I personally would find worrisome about buying it. I pointed out the slope in the hardwood floor, the crack in the front bedroom wall, and then - kindly, reluctantly – I handed him Bert Graystone's report complete with graphs, drawings, and those appalling figures totaling $70,000. "At least," I added, shrugging in sympathy.

By the time I had handed out three reports, the broker arrived. He was legally required to disclose the report to all prospective buyers. There was only a trickle of people. Many details later, my fine new fattened offer looked pretty good, and the house was mine. I paid the balloon payment off to Kori and Steve a year and a half later, well ahead of time, when I refinanced. Angels.

As I lie on my plastic reclining lawn chair, the blue jays hop boldly to the glass table to enjoy dip into the wild birdseed. Fixing the nearby cats with their shiny black onyx eyes, they shake their spiky punk topknots, with the emphatic blue neon stripes, and squawk. I see that the jasmine vine I planted years ago and thought was dead, tender hors-d'oeuvres for the deer, has made its way up to the top of the dark shiny green leaves of the *pittosporum*. *Jasmine officinale*, poet's jasmine, has burst into blossom, a frothing abundance of white flowers that coat me like scented butter. Who would think that such a delicate beautiful thing could be so powerful? And how patience and staying close to the bone until it is safe, following whatever urge to keep going and climb, would turn out so magnificently? A pair of hummingbirds, one with coppery red throat, both in iridescent green bodies, whirr above, dart and dive from the honeysuckle to the desert sage, then stop, hovering, to bless us below.

As Bonnie Raitt said, "It took me a long time to get here but I'm right on time."

Listening With the Ear of Your Heart

All month a stag has been here, clicking down the wooden stairs to stride down the middle of Shasta Road, kingly. Or lying in the pile of red and orange leaves on top of the garage roof, noble gaze of shining onyx surveying the ordinary world with dignified reserve. His olive gray fur blends into the gnarled root branches of the dead rosemary as he polishes his antlers, making the hanging bushes bounce. Now he sits, watching, still, until I move into the kitchen and he closes his eyes, slowly chewing.

He has appeared like magic, like the answer to an unasked question. Yesterday, he was lying comfortably under the kitchen window next to the coiled green hose, just outside the French doors. I think he enjoys jazz. Susannah McCorkle was singing Cole Porter tunes. He was still there an hour later, listening to Don Pullen on piano, "Evidence of Things Unseen."

I wonder if he is one of the twin fawns three years ago who woke me up at dawn, chasing each other in a nimble game of tag as their mother, annoyed, nipped at their white flag tails. His antlers, reminiscent of the world tree, connect us to the spirit of sky, body of earth, and underworld where we are rooted. In Celtic legend, his antlers acted like divining rods to find the energy lines of the earth. Isn't that our task, too? To align ourselves, our personal energies with those of the earth? Some of the worst effects of the mining and drilling practices of industry have created imbalances in the earth's grid, interrupting and blocking earth's energy flows. What holes have been drilled in our own lives, what cutting of mountains and clearing of forests have moved us away from our energy?

I think of the headaches, the sinus infections, drilling me for months. Making me attend to the place right behind my eyes, and the blocking of my third eye sight. Maybe I need to grow some antlers! As protection for my eyes. As antennae to the spirit world. Or at least use some of the glucosamine in them to boost my immune system.

This morning the stag was snuffling through the birdseed on the patio bricks, finding the corn. He paused to rub his black, satin nose across his olive grey flank. Then his head was up, listening, nostrils quivering. Perhaps it is my reflection that has put him on alert, or the grinding of coffee beans. I pick up an organic Fuji apple and roll it towards him, gently across the ground.

My yard is now fenced on three sides by neighbors. One is a chain link fence that closes off a barren backyard full of machinery, tools, car parts. Nothing lives there. It feels like a prison yard. What kinds of unnatural borders are drawn around the world, lines deciding where you belong, who the enemies are, where the wars will be cast. I struggle for breath. This green hillside and red stone patio a shrunken refuge, retreat, hideaway, for the remaining city crowded wild animals. And me. Sacred ground. The ground where inner and outer realities overlap, the place where we are both embodied and holy. The stag moves easily between the living and the dream worlds, especially at Samhain, the Celtic New Year. This is the time of no-time, when the veils are thinnest.

His place is at the edge of wildness. Sometimes, he sits at the top of the stairs outside where I can see his antlers gently swaying as I walk up to the house. The other morning as I headed down the stairs to my car, he was there watching the street. Calmly, he looked up at me, his legs gracefully folded underneath. I began to talk to him, explain how I was sorry to disturb him but I had to go to my office, the only way to my car was down these stairs. He didn't move. I didn't really want to go to the office, or perhaps into the world, the marketplace. I was at the third step down before he moved, and I'm not sure it was a threshold I should have walked over. Can I remember what is holy, bring this beauty and magic into that other ordinary world?

The stag has shown me the way to proceed before, appearing in a dream thirty years ago. I had one of many nightmares about being all alone, a divorced mother, lost.

The dream began:

I'm in a city multi- level parking garage, with low ceilings, concrete floors, and steel caged lifts. I couldn't find my car, or my keys. After going up and down all the levels I finally left the garage, and the city, and wandered out into the undeveloped grassy land behind the buildings and houses. I was looking in the tall yellow grass for my keys, digging with a stick, when a stag silently revealed himself to me, slowly, like magic appearing out of nowhere. He lowered his great gentle head and with his antlers pointed to the ground to show me how to search for the way, his antlers antennae to the spirit world. Without words he said 'Listen with the ear of your heart and you'll find your path.'

Turning to the voice of the earth, the voice that beats in the deep pulse of the womb of the earth, listening to our own inner voice, is the way to proceed for us all. There we find the seeds of new life.

Every single culture in the world originated in shamanism. Yet we have been so cut off from our own creative transformative energies, the wellsprings of wisdom. Turning down to the mysteries of the dark and our deepest hearts, we find ourselves beating with the heart of the world. The world of human integrity is a green world. We must learn how to restore vitality to our desiccated souls.

After an unleashed dog chased the stag up the hill yesterday morning, I feared he would not return. But last night, I heard him, crackling through the dry slick oak leaves. The clunk of a hoof against a rock. The full moon shone like a pearl, faintly pink, over the lace of the eucalyptus tree. I imagined his horns silhouetted as the tree of life, holding the moon like a cradle. Tomorrow, the rays of the rising sun will slide over his antlers like honey. In this long season of darkness, he comes as messenger walking with our ancestors' souls, the laws of the land, the law of love.

As I take my tea and plate of honeyed bread out to the patio, I see the stag pawing the dust under the Queensland *pittosporum* tree, making a bed to nap. While I sit reading and writing, he rouses himself, moves slowly behind the rosemary bushes and down the stairs. I hold my breath, keep my eyes down. Click click over the patio bricks, his black nose moist, his eyes steady. He lowers his head to the ground for the corn, then up to the table where I sit. I can see out of the corner of my eye the lichen -like covering between his horns, but it's not green. It's gold.

Speckled with gold. His tongue comes out to lick the glass tabletop, for the corn I have laid out. His head is bent to keep the antlers out of the way, but they are also bent towards me, lending me his fearlessness, this spiritual pathfinder, this gentle warrior who integrates masculine and feminine energies. Showing me that life's mysteries, usually hidden, want to be seen and known. We seek a wild peace.

In the Beginning Was a Song

"The cure for anything is salt water:

sweat, tears, or the sea."

- Isak Dinesen

This morning I woke up to a birdsong chorale after a rainy night. There are so many singing, twittering, whistling birds, a glee club warming up. The moist air is dense with life and spirit. A symphony tuning its instruments.

It reminds me of the undersea sounds of the whales and dolphins on my recent Hawaii trip. I was just there six months ago. But since then I've had almost continuous sinus headaches and three infections that drove me to the clinic and $30-a-pill antibiotics. The nurse practitioner said I had untreated allergies. I stopped eating wheat, again. Got a CO monitor to check the old wall heaters. Moved out of my airless bedroom and possible dust mite reservation of a bed to sleep in the living room on the couch, under open windows and close to the trees. Washed my sinuses daily with a saline solution in a little Neti pot in the shape of an elephant head. Began yoga. Doubled up on acupuncture. The constant forehead thrum of headache, my burning head, burrowed me in despair. I decided I was allergic to my life.

I had put "whale-watching" on my wish list for more years than I want to admit. This is the year, and Maui is the whale-watching capital, which apparently thousands of other people know too. I found out the hotels and airlines were almost completely booked for the annual whale festivals. I got the last seat on the (now out of business) ATA plane, and a hotel room on the Kaanapali shore. Four stories up, with a slanted view of a little waterfall and koi pond, and windows that don't open, keeping me boxed in without sound or breezes. I try a few yoga poses, downward dog, but the headache lingers. After a walk on the beach I enter the ocean. The cool water slides over my head like a soothing hand, a baptism. The headache is gone.

Later, as I sit in the hotel lobby next to an ancient Hawaiian canoe with my latte and journal, I spot a beautiful gray-blue stone statue of a bird next to the little waterfall garden where tourists are having their pictures taken. It is large and squat, its head tucked into its white-and-blue body. What a lovely work of art. How did I not notice it before? At that moment a wind comes up, *ha*, like a breath, and three thin white feathers rise up like a plume. Like the plume of the whale's breath. It's alive! Holding on for dear life. *Auku'u*, a black-crowned night heron. She clings to the small lava rock with her yellow feet, hunched down in this small green oasis in the middle of the strip of condos and tall hotels, manicured lawns, the plastic swimming pool ten feet from the ocean where the hotel guests cluster, hunkered down in their sterile, windless, and chlorinated fort.

I find her honored in the Hawaiian creation chant,

the *Kumilipo*:

Man born for the narrow stream,

Woman for the broad stream

Born was the *Auku'u,* living by the sea,

Guarded by the *Ekupu'u*, bird living on land.

It is the god who enters, not as a human does he enter.

(Translated by Kamuela Lindsay)

The *auku'u* fixes her red eyes on the huge golden koi circling the small pond. A waterfall trickles past the bit of scarlet bougainvillea, the palm fronds. Perhaps she clings to the memories of the old stories held in the once liquid fires of the lava. I, too, have flown hundreds of miles—though not under my own wings—to find a *kipuka,* an oasis in the middle of the fire. A *kipuka* is an area of land around which lava flows - it is spared the burial and incineration of Pele's embrace.

I needed a wilderness watering spot for my soul, an opening in the suffocating fog of financial obligations and newspaper pictures of bombed children and anguished parents, ruined lands and decimated animal species.

Trying to hold on to sanity and remember being human, that we stand ultimately on joy, in beauty, together.

What is native to being human?

Here in Lahaina Bay, the six or seven thousand humpback whales that have swum down from Alaska to calve and to mate swim peacefully in the calm, warm waters. A mother and calf practice arching their silvery backs out of the water, the blows of exhalation misting at 300 miles an hour. Next to our cruise boat is a small, brilliant yellow raft, with six or so people sitting on the edge with their feet hanging over the side. The mother-calf pair approach and circle again and again, with their tons of friendly curiosity.

As we head out to sea, the pilot begins to chant a *mele*, a song that announces us as meaning no harm. The *mele* asks for permission to enter the ocean, acknowledging and appreciating the animals, plants, and coral that reside in the sea. We come as guests, with respect. As if answering our request, a spinner dolphin bounds toward our bow, smiling, then drops back to join his friends, who travel at our side for an hour to Molokini, the crescent-shaped volcanic crater that protects the coral reefs and their dwellers. Snorkeling, there are dozens of brilliant yellow fish with black stripes, a teardrop butterfly fish called *Lau-Hau*. A fancier one with a thin trailing fin like a feather, "Moorish Idol," *kihikihi*. Beneath this swirl of fish glide a few large pastel ones in pinks, turquoise, pale green, yellow, with a dramatic black tail – *Hinalea luahine*.

Back on the boat we watch the distant plumes of white water near Kahoolawe in silence as we hear the story of this little island. Named for the whales, *kohola*, it was bombed by the United States military for decades as "practice." In 1994, there was a ceremony to return the island to the Hawaiians, who are slowly removing the land mines and unexploded bombs so it will be safe. The ceremony celebrates the surviving sacredness of the land in spite of the years of violation.

The first of three cruises I scheduled is a stargazing trip on the night of the Chinese Lunar New Year with a resident astronomer. Fortunate to have the first clear night in two weeks of rain, we are mesmerized listening to the rich information of millions and billions, years and miles and galaxies, intent on locating Orion's Belt, the Seven Sisters of the Pleiades, when we hear a loud "whoosh" right next to us. What was that? Again, "whoosh," as the stargazing whale sighs with us. The crew drops a microphone into the water so we can hear what is going on, who is there. I think we might hear a single note or echo. Instead, a carnival, a festival, a barnyard of squeaks and rumbles and clucks and bellows. Call and counterpoint. Chorale. A mournful dirge. A hymn that traces the genealogy of the species, the *himeni,* the hymns. A reverberating dissonance. Then a sonorous, thundering tone, on and on for many minutes. We learn that only the males sing, and different populations around the world sing different songs, which are always, slowly, changing in structure and sequence. Their songs are like poems of transformation, like the Hawaiian language, with its words ending in vowels, is always open to the next change.

On another boat the following day, green sea turtles bob next to our boat with their pointy beaks and exotic, slanted eyes, holding 75 million years of memory. When we are snorkeling I spot a green sea turtle and follow her, swimming above her carapace the exact color of the seaweed, the corals, in mottled dark brown with radiating wavy markings of olive and black. The sand and silt that stir around her remind me of the earth that Turtle Mother carries on her back in the myths of many native peoples. She carries the earth on her back to support us all, linking us also to the moon by the thirteen segments of her shell, fragmented yet bound together as a whole circle. This kind of turtle cannot draw her flippers or head under her shell, destined to ride the waves with her neck stuck out.

The Greeks pictured Aphrodite, born out of the foam of the sea, goddess of beauty, love, and joy, with green sea turtles. What can *honu,* the sea turtle, teach us about that?

She represents the feminine principle. Longevity and the uniting of heaven, her shell, with earth, her body. Peace. Perseverance. Wisdom. The slow steadiness of journey that honors completion, wholeness, and harmony. As she cannot separate herself from her shell, neither can we separate ourselves from the earth.

The way to heaven is through the earth.

What is our part? The native human? To know that everything is alive and has a spirit of its own. Everything is connected and dependent on each other. Everything is constantly changing, like a song, like the open mouth that sings. To know these things and to make an offering. The Hawaiian word for flat land, the Earth, is *honua; ho*—to give or transfer; *nua*—to make noise, cough, coo like a dove, grunt like a pig. As each of us gives away a little of ourselves and makes a sound, we make the land, create the world.

The whales know their way home. They sing their thousands of miles of journey in community, joyfully leaping and birthing and transforming themselves season after season.

Do we have a song to sing together? One that is strong enough to carry us all our lives?

Marrying My Soul Mate

The green wooden door to the laundry room downstairs is hammering its uneven rhythm, the wind crackling across the wet sky like rippling sheet metal, and rain slickening everything green. I am happy to be in my blue flannel pajamas with white clouds, listening to Norah Jones sing. I don't know why her voice makes me cry, or maybe it's the words: "Human kindness, overflowing, and I think it's going to rain today."

Last night I went to a musician friend's concert at

the school in Lagunitas, out in San Geronimo Valley, on the road to Point Reyes. It was a family affair, with three generations of singers, drummers, guitar and cello players performing. The Master of Ceremonies was my friend's son, a young man of about twenty with Down's syndrome. He has done this role for years, in his bright red jacket, his enthusiasm for the show, the music, demonstrated in his booming voice and rocking out dance moves. The room was packed. Everyone got a standing ovation. Everyone was a star. Aren't we all?

Years ago, astronomers discovered that dark clouds of matter far out in the Milky Way are strewn with billions of tiny diamonds. Aren't we made of this dust? Aren't we diamonds? There is a Hubble picture of a galaxy in the Milky Way that looks like a gold ring encrusted with a diamond star. We are precious like that.

When I turned fifty, I wanted to certify that I was indeed precious. It was looking very unlikely that I would marry again, wear a diamond ring on my left hand. But my dear old friend Linda Lee, a college sorority sister, had been dealing in diamonds for years as a jewelry maker. She now called herself Lulu, and lived in New York City with her third, much younger husband. When I found out

Lulu's gold and diamond jewelry was being displayed at the new Barney's in Los Angeles, I decided to take my two teenage daughters down for my birthday celebration. I'd buy myself a diamond. Marry myself to my own future. Plight my troth to creativity and a soulful life.

Like most creative women, Linda Lee had traveled a weaving road. At UC Berkeley, she was renown as a campus beauty, a queen. Tall and willowy, her huge green eyes shone with hopeful longing. In a perfect harmony of form, even her feet were beautiful. She was also very generous, brilliant, and lonely. We married Phi Gamma Delta brothers, and followed our husbands to their jobs in Washington, D.C. We didn't have an honest conversation until after we were both divorced fifteen years later.

Lulu became an actress, first at Berkeley Rep then in New York. But after years of struggle, traveling in community theater and another divorce, she had taken to sleeping all day in her Soho loft swaddled in her leather jacket. One morning her cleaning lady Edna found her crying in bed.

"Miss Linda Lee, you have got to find you a job that pays you some money. What are you going to do? What do you want to do?"

"Make jewelry."

"Well why don't you do it?"

"I don't have the money."

Edna loaned her $200 for the class. Master welders told Linda Lee she couldn't do what she envisioned, put all those diamonds in gold, but she persisted, and is an extremely successful jewelry maker.

Arriving at Barney's, Susannah, Azzia and I went past the valets and chauffeurs to the front counters. The precious jewelry section looked like museum showcases. Lulu's pieces bold, elegant solid gold bands, 24 carat, in different shades of yellow and white, set with diamonds all the way around. They each had mythological names according to the slightly varied styles. I chose "Leda," loving the image of the swan, and the circle of four diamonds. Just enough. A number of wholeness, completion. After trying one on, I decided two would be better. I would marry myself to my spiritual life and creative path whether or not I ever wore a wedding band again. As I tried them on, I told the saleslady about my long ago friendship with Linda Lee, now Lulu. The girls were thrilled, cheering me on. As I was taking in an acceptance of my partnerless state and joy in my new beautiful, creative life, the manager came out with a strange look on her face.

"Lulu is on the phone and wants to talk to you." Shaking her head in dismay, she said

"We never talk to her on the phone, she's way too busy. She doesn't even have voicemail."

But there she was. By chance. By synchronicity. By grace. I was so excited to talk to her, and she to me, and for us to celebrate how far we'd come, how much we loved each other even after such a long separation. We had been through so many changes, losses, detours, and yet we were still here. More than ever, ourselves. The two rings on my right hand felt grounding, anchoring me to an inner compass that would serve me faithfully.

Several years later, when I got a cancer diagnosis, my most encouraging guidance came from those rings as they appeared in a dream:

I am driving across a lake, over a wooden bridge on a starless and black moon night. Somehow I drive over the edge, through the railing, and am flung into the black water miles away from anybody. My rings fall off and sink to the bottom. As I give into despair and certain death, suddenly the scene shifts. It is now the middle of the day. Fishermen call out merrily from their rowboats. Children and a golden dog swim in the lake, and there are picknickers on the shore. The place teems with life. Someone hands me back my rings. They have changed. Instead of single bands with several diamonds they are as thick as the length of my fingers, and as dense with diamonds as the Milky Way is brimming with stars.

I knew I was going to survive the surgery and the cancer, and I did. There is no distinction between the world outside and the world inside. Our continuing dialogue with God takes place in both worlds. We are all diamonds.

As Hildegard of Bingen says,

"There is no creation that does not have a radiance, be it greenness or seed, blossom or beauty. It could not be creation without it."

Singing in Tree

"We must come to the end
before a new beginning can come to us."
- Helene Cixous

Sitting in the backyard, I marvel at this unnamed plant, found on the nursery table under a sign: "For Hummingbirds and Bees." Its narrow, bright-green stem stretches up almost five feet, doing absolutely nothing for the first couple of feet. Or perhaps pruned by the deer. Finally, yesterday, at the very top, a thistle. A round ball maybe two inches across, with spikes sticking out. On either side of the stem, perfectly symmetrical pairs of toothed leaves mirror each other. Today, the thistle has burst into a cascade of pale, peach tubes. Like rows of dreadlocks, they spill over a pair of long, smooth leaves that twirl in the breeze like dancers legs pirouetting. Who could have imagined the mysteries of this plant, that it had such apricot exuberance to express in such adverse conditions?

Twenty years ago, writing my dissertation, I was struggling with the dryness of my excessively intellectual voice. This dream helped to move me in the direction of a deeper intelligence, toward my wild feminine soul and an ecology of self:

I enter an old, elegant theater - maybe an auditorium - from the doors at the top, the back. There are tiers of seats covered in a richly textured, deep-rose satin. The floor is slanted at a steep angle to the stage, the ceiling carved alive with ornate gold scrolls. Mother and I are supposed to do a performance together - a duet. I am late, scrambling down the aisle to get to the stage where she stands, impatient, lips pursed and eyes narrowed. She has some papers in her hands – our script, our lines, the score for the music we are to sing. She hands me my copy. I stare at the sheet of music, aware that we will be singing a cappella. I vaguely remember we have sung this music for many, many years. There is a faint scent of memory, of nostalgia, like a familiar childhood hymn or nursery rhyme. We have rehearsed this piece so many times. But to my horror, I no longer understand the music or the lyrics. I cannot remember the tune. The words are all in Latin - the language of the church, the priests, the fathers. They no longer make sense.

Mother is perfectly calm and begins to sing, holding out the music for me to see. I stare and stare. The black words and lines of the score slowly pale, dissolving until the paper is a white void. As I concentrate, trying to read what is fading from sight, a faint image begins to rise out of the very texture of the paper, as part of the fabric, its pulp developing slowly like a photograph. Gradually, a dense woods emerges, with large, deep-green trees, lush with leaves. These are very old oaks. One of the trees grows to fill out the entire page to its edges, the pulp and color and shape all in one. This is the new song.

How am I going to sing in Tree?

We were singing different songs. I had forgotten the old songs she had taught me, the church had taught me, and now I had to find the new song. Mother was very upset with me in the dream, as she has been in waking life, because I can no longer sing the song of the Fathers or obey the laws of a hierarchy of priests.

When the feminine was part of the worldview, the tree was the Tree of Knowledge, the World Tree, or axis mundi at the center of the earth. Uniting the three realms of heaven, earth, and the underworld, the sacred tree had the power to reveal messages from the gods. As a symbol of the self in the process of becoming, the tree unites the opposites of masculine and feminine, conscious mind and unconscious knowing. It challenges us to undertake the journey of spiritual transformation. We must first understand our connection to the earth and the seasons of our lives, the cycles of the moon and the language of the Mother tongue.

"If we surrendered to earth's intelligence
we could rise up rooted, like trees."
- Rainer Maria Rilke

I want to sing a woman's song, from the womb mysteries of Mother Earth and my true nature. We have all been cut off from our roots and the wells of creative transformation, those energies that lie in the mysteries of the dark. Knowledge of the divine begins in nature, which indigenous people remember, and alchemical and Celtic traditions knew. Black Elk, the Native American visionary, described many sacred hoops connecting the peoples of the world. In one vision a single great tree, flowering and beautiful, shelters all the children of the earth. It is time to restore that tree to the world. A tree of dreams, a tree of beauty, a tree of God, a tree of enlightened self.

My dream image of the tree shows us there is no separation between its roots in darkness, its flowering to the sky. No separation from its growing and the paper out of which it emerges, the paper from its own body: a mandala, a symbol of wholeness. The greening power of God.

To restore the world we must re-story the world. Without the salmon, the redwoods die. Without the forests, the earth will die. Trees are the lungs of the earth. They rain upward, keeping the earth moist. A grove of quaking aspen is a single organism that sends out runners, each putting down roots over thousands of acres, sending up shoots of new leaves. We, too, are connected to every living thing. When we truly know that, we will understand the fierce urgency of our decisions to save the trees.

The tree is the backbone of the world Goddess. The fruit of the mother tree, the rose apple—wisdom. The rhythms of nature are our own. The oak is a symbolic doorway to the mysteries, reminding us of the need to make ascents and descents in our evolutionary spiral path to become our truest selves, earthed and rooted in the laws of our own nature. The roots stretch down to the waters of life, the reservoirs of feminine renewal, and the gifts of going down into the dark.

There is a living book of holy wisdom in the dream world, in the world of nature, and in science that teaches us about our interconnection and infinitely creative unfolding.

How to sing in Tree? Our estrangement from nature, from the laws of our own nature, is healed by honoring our bodies as we honor the land. The way for personal, individual transformation is also the way to cultural transformation. The rediscovery of the heart of joy.

I dream:

I walk alone up to the hills above the city. The golden wheel of the sun has turned again, bringing the light of a new dawn. The beekeepers have returned, or rather, the bees have returned, and the dozens of hives are being tended to by beekeepers in their netted hats and gloves. Tending to the queen, to community, to the sweetness of life. I walk along the ridge, a little afraid I'll be stung but I'm not. The hills are so green below and the forest abundant behind. I take off flying over the valley, the city, exhilarated, fearless.

Life in the Round

"In the beginning was thought, and her name was Woman…She is the Old Woman Spider who weaves us together in a fabric of interconnection."

- Paula Gunn Allen, *The Sacred Hoop*

There are rows of rain clouds blossoming along the horizon like white winter peonies. Above them float two grey winged clouds looking like eagle shadows. A string of raindrops hangs on a spider web like pearls, each one a glistening world of its own. And yet, each one also reflects every other sparkling jewel in a glittering lacework of water.

On the radio, Claude Bolling and Yo-Yo Ma are playing a tune called "Baroque in Rhythm." The yearning of the cello seems to question: *Do you, do you ever wonder why you're here?* and the jazz piano dances alongside. Eventually they move into a joyful ragtime. So many levels of meaning, from Bach to boogie-woogie, weaving a rich tapestry of vibrations and rhythms and feelings. Not visible but felt, like the gossamer web of relationships that connects us all to this universe, and the life of the planet.

We once knew our place in nature and the mystery of a world ensouled, imagined as the Great Mother. Far from this knowing of *Anima Mundi*, thousands of years away from the feminine principle, we became soul-sick and gravely harmed our beautiful planet. This morning in the news, hundreds of seabirds, cormorants, grebes and loons, are found dead along the California coast. Many of them are emaciated. There is less food in the ocean for the orcas. And for us. We have forgotten what it means to be human, to be connected to wildness.

"The ecological holocaust is twofold: it has to do with the gross overuse of our external environment, and the incredible underuse of our internal environment." - Jean Houston

We must go down to the roots, the mythic traditions

where we all began. It is time to become a culture of dreamers, to awaken to the ecology of self we need. To listen to the emergent wisdom of the dynamic, transformative feminine.

Twenty years ago Grandmother Spider Woman presented herself to me in a dream:

My youngest daughter Azzia is three, or perhaps four. I take her outside to show her the beauties and joys of nature. We hold hands, meander at the slow pace of wonder. In our exploring, we begin to find things on the ground to look at, to pick up. Stones, a gracefully shaped twig, a burnt ocher leaf. Earthworms come out of the ground, and she picks a fleshy one up to admire it. I try to be enthusiastic in spite of being a bit repulsed. The first worms that come up are plain, ordinary brown and pinkish worms, but the next batch are spotted, and striped, in many different colors. Fascinated, we pick them up to see their marvelous patterns.

A spider emerges out of the ground, a plain, thin, wiry Daddy Longlegs. The next spider is thicker, brown, a common household spider. A black spider with red dots, and all kinds of colors and patterns. Then a furry tarantula sidles over. I stifle a shudder and summon my courage to let the spider crawl on my arm. Azzia isn't afraid, only curious.

Then a wondrous black spider comes strolling along. She is as big as a huge, ancient tortoise, with two cobalt blue silk antennae on either side of her head. They are almost transparent and can turn to all sides to see, like periscopes. Behind these delicate antennae are large pink feathers. On her back, near the end of her, are many soft, large white plumes. She is a stunning, glorious creature! Pausing for a moment, she then heads off purposefully down the dirt path to our left which leads into a dark, dense forest. She expects us to follow. I do not hesitate. As we leave, I see my father to the right. He sits in a chair in the middle of a clearing, a place shorn of all living things. He is reading a book. "Father!" I call. "Look at this fantastic spider!" But he is engrossed in his book. By the time he looks up, she has passed by him, and we are following into the forest.

The Father sits in his chair, above the earth, separated and impenetrable like a Newtonian atom. There is an illusion of control, of order. If his identity depends on this perimeter, connection will feel like a threat. He avoids the chaos of wildness, of his own feelings. Yet it is out of chaos that new order emerges, so he misses what he seeks. In the clear-cut barren emptiness limited to a narrow intellect, there is not enough to green our souls.

What is the path into the forest? And who was it

calling me, calling us as mother and daughter, deep into the wilderness? We were called by the unknown, the mystery, the holy, the numinous. The feminine way of knowing demands going into darkness, learning to live with chaos, finding the threads of meaning and pattern out of our own living. Opening to life, to the extravagant wealth of reality. We must learn how to stretch between opposites. Bear the darkness and love the light. Create a work of art, our lives, out of our own substance.

We need to reweave the broken web of our being. By doing so, we can remake the world. See ourselves from the earth up rather than the sky down. Understand that we are mostly empty space, more liquid than solid, and always becoming. We are the universe in person, of the earth not on it. We carry the ashes of stars in our bones, we look out through seawater. The spark of life that animates each of us was first lit at the dawn of creation.

The shift we need to bring to our consciousness is not only from a mechanistic view to a holistic one, but from a timeless universe to an evolving and creative one. As part of a planetary web of consciousness, the *noosphere* that Teilhard de Chardin described, all minds are evolving together. Joseph Campbell, at the end of his life, told us we needed a new planetary mythology, one based on the crisis and conditions of our times. In both science and religion, we have lived with a mythology of fragmentation for thousands of years. The most powerful and pervasive source of fragmentation is the identification of our individual selves as absolute, separate, and distinct from others. We now know this is a mistaken and dangerous idea. It has fostered devastation, destruction and despair throughout the world. By withdrawing from nature and the material world a sense of the sacred, we have poisoned the wellwaters of the land and the wellspring of our souls.

What's being lost is almost everything.

The problems of both psychology and ecology are worldview problems.

"The transformation of our worldview necessitates the transformation of our view of the feminine."

- James Hillman

When we reconnect to the dynamic, transformative feminine, we restore our connection to the natural world and also to our own souls.

Together with ancient indigenous intellectual and religious traditions, with the sacred feminine, and new science, we can re-imagine our world. There are new myths emerging to seed the future. And new songs to sing it all into being.

The world of female integrity is a green world. We must honor the authority of wildness.

The time is now. Leading us is the wisdom of the grandmothers in the various ways they are appearing to us. Grandmother Spider Woman is the universe dreaming, dreaming us into loving the beauty of the world. I think she has been telling stories to the physicists, who believe that we are all vibrations, vibrating strings interacting with each other. The universe is more like a symphony than a corporation of matter. As we learn about string theory, perhaps we can take in the picture of a universe that is not only like a web but like a great stringed instrument, a dynamic vibrating instrument, and we each have a song to play.

We vibrate in the energy waves of probabilities shimmering in the multiple dimensions of being, until an act of observation or engagement precipitates them into the particle nature of things. It is our responsibility to participate as co-creators. In Hawaiian the word *kuleana,* has an especially apt meaning of responsibility: own your gifts and share them with the world. It is especially time for the women to come forth. They are the ones we've been waiting for, and the men who understand and honor the sacred feminine.

"It is no coincidence that creativity and the feminine come forth together. Creative individuals in this culture are called upon to abandon the masculine ground of collective consciousness and descend to the mother-realm in order to bring forth what demands to be born into the new age."

- Janet Dallett

The old structures - economic, social, political -are dissolving. We are at a bifurcation point where the system can either shift, leap into a new pattern that is more inclusive and complex, or collapse into death. It is the new feminine archetype - the dynamic, transformative principle - that is leading the way. Eventually, after the old structures have dissolved, there will be a breakthrough to a new order, a new pattern that connects. We the women are the pilgrims and pioneers, the midwives and the mothers of this new emerging world.

Ever unfolding, we are extravagant beings, as rich and complex as the world outside. When we truly understand our interconnection and the fragility of our shared web of life, we will have peace.

Blossom Afire

This summer morning, I'm sitting in the backyard where the baby deer have come, curious, and the green gold hummingbird clicks in delight at the new potted salvia – "Red Hot Sally." This is the world as it should be, peaceful and beautiful, a lot different from what goes on out there, in the front yard, down the driveway, by the road. When I came home last night, climbed back into the green sheltered world of ivy and laurel, I caught sight of a brilliant red spot out of the corner of my eye. I've planted nothing there, I thought, only the self-sustaining green of wild and chance trees and shrubs. Backing up, I spy a three blossomed, three headed, huge brilliant red amaryllis. What a lovely surprise, Christmas gift leftover. How in the world did it get there?

Puzzled, I walked up the rest of the stairs and into my room before I remember, sitting at my writing table overlooking the Bay, what had happened one morning months ago. Still in my pajamas, writing down the dreams of the night before a horn honked. Once. Twice. I live in the city, I can tolerate a few honks, the occasional over-vigilant car or house alarm. It's never danger, just technology run amok without enough to do. Then there was a third, long, drawn out honk. Irritated, I went to the deck. It was a Monday morning, recycling day. I peered over the railing to see a fat white man pushing on his horn, behind the - beloved - recycling truck. There was no place for the truck to go, and the city worker was rapidly picking up the cheery blue baskets which I think of as a little bitty offerings to care for Mother Earth.

I yelled at the man to cut it out, but tightly windowed in his Lexus bubble he couldn't hear me. I didn't want to go down in my pajamas, but I was fiery with rage. Pele of the volcanoes! I grabbed the nearest unbreakable object - a plastic pot filled with dirt. I flung it at the car, but the pot hit the laurel branches and all the dirt fell out. With, apparently, the Christmas amaryllis. The pot missed his car, and tumbled down the street with a faint clatter.

It's another Christmas season, and my rage is blooming. In the paper, and all the news channels, the story of the Newtown shootings of twenty first graders and six protective school staffers at Sandy Hook Elementary School cracks our hearts open. We imagine the very few minutes of gunshots, as teachers tried to shepherd their little charges into cupboards, closets, or in their arms. The long day as the surviving children were reunited with their parents at the firehouse. Gradually, as families reunited, there were twenty families left. Waiting. Perhaps there was still hope. Injured children at the hospital, or run into the woods. But there were no more children coming. In a merciful moment, Connecticut Governor Dannel Malloy broke with protocol, not waiting for the Medical Examiner to give a final count. He went to the firehouse and told the parents, the families, there would be no more children coming. And then they had to leave the children, shot multiple times each, in their classrooms. All night.

Whatever the complex reasons for this mass shooting, several things are true. The gun the shooter used was a Bushmaster AR 15, an assault weapon, first used in Vietnam, that you can now buy at Walmart. An ad for this particular gun, also used in last year's Aurora movie theater shooting, and an Oregon shopping mall, reads "Consider your man card reissued." There will always be a few mentally ill people. But it is this culture that creates and values a particular male ideal, a particular valuing of profits regardless of the meaning and purposes of the goods and services sold.

What is the business of our country if not to take care of its people, especially the children? What is the real cost to all of us, including the 30,000 people killed each year by gun violence? The tens of thousands wounded, disabled, traumatized, in need of extensive medical care.

As a country, we show this face to the world.

U.S. arms exports account for more than half of total global arms deliveries. We are the largest arms dealer in the world, and have been for many years.

While boasting about democracy, security and peace, we sell weapons to dictators, human rights abusers and countries at war or at the edge of war, sometimes with each other.

The U.S. has repeatedly refused to sign the Convention of Cluster Munitions, which bans the use of cluster bombs and has been signed by 100 other countries. In fact, we recently petitioned the United Nations to suspend this ban. Cluster bombs have a long-lived capacity to cause damage, mainly to civilians. Children find them in the ground unexploded and are frequently killed or maimed. There are a few rays of hope with our current President. Obama is the first American President to make nuclear disarmament a centerpiece of American defense policy. He negotiated a nuclear disarmament treaty with Russia in 2010, and has declared his intention to get some common sense gun regulation to prevent further massacres at home.

We as a country are responsible for terrible human rights abuses at Abu Ghraib, Guantanamo Bay, wars abroad, and the ever-expanding prison system. Our history with indigenous peoples is one of genocide, thievery of culture and land, decimating Native Americans and Hawaiian populations.

These arms deals do not foster security or stability in the world. Is this who we truly are? Is this the country we want to be? Our actions define us as a bully, sometimes working directly and other times through finance and supplies of other bullies.

Can we imagine power as peace? We have a choice.

Always a choice. The truth is so, so simple. I am dizzy in its absence: take care of the babies, save the children.

At a government peace summit years ago, an ambassador suggested that the warring sides hand a baby around, just hand a baby around the negotiating table and see what comes to mind. Or bring the women, the mothers and grandmothers to the circle. Better yet, let them run it.

In this last national election, more women were elected to Congress than ever before. Voters were buoyed by impassioned reactions to the GOP war on women, and ready to see better ideology and policy decisions in government. We now have twenty woman Senators, seventy-six women State Representatives. I want to see and hear more wild wisdom and women's voices, which are still dismally represented in the business world. I want to see feminine power ignited. Not in the pink pretty limp "naked lady" amaryllis struggling out of barren dirt, but the fiery red heart of this beauty in my front yard. Standing tall out of the green lush forest, coming out of hiding from the shadows of the tree trunks, a two-foot high green backbone, speaking with the authority of wildness.

"The future of the world depends on women."

- Kofi Annan, Director General, United Nations

"Love is much more demanding than law."

- Archbishop Desmond Tutu

Can we love this world into a wild peace?

Seven Trees and Half the World's Children

Here's what's running through my mind, as Tommy Flanagan plays "Peace" on the radio. How inextricably linked are the survival of our wild places and the survival of our children. There is a picture in the San Francisco Chronicle of 94-year-old Sylvia McLaughlin planting the 100,000th seedling of native wetland plants as part of the restoration of the shoreline. In 1961, she, along with Kay Kerr and Esther Gulick, founded the Save San

Francisco Bay Association. The Bay was on its way to becoming a river. It was ringed with garbage dumps, burning tires. Raw sewage ran untreated into its waters. And almost every year after that, there have various public and private plans to develop the shoreline, ruining the wetlands and shrinking space for wildlife. My father, Dwight Steele, worked closely with Save the Bay and Sylvia, as do many other fierce and brilliant environmentalists. But these three women began a grassroots environmental organization when there were few women visible in leadership. Filling the Bay was considered economic progress. Now future children are able to enjoy the Bay waters, to appreciate the burrowing owls, the black-tailed jackrabbits, the ducks and the egrets. They can thrive in healthy relationship to nature right next door to their urban neighborhoods.

On the wall behind my computer, I have a picture of Nobel Peace Prize winner Wangari Maathai with her arms spread wide, grinning, in a brilliant orange traditional draped dress and tied turban scarf. Exuberant, she told the audience in Oslo that protecting the world's resources was linked to halting violence. "We are called to assist the Earth to heal her wounds, and in the process heal our own," she said. Seven trees, and the Green Belt Movement began. They planted seeds for peace, seeded our hope for the future.

She was the first African woman to win the Nobel Peace Prize, the first environmentalist to win. She planted seven trees in Kenya 1977; now there are 51 million as a result of her movement. Kenya was ruled by a dictator, and a culture of violence permeated the villages and households. She was trying to save the shrinking forests, to get firewood for the impoverished rural women. In teaching them to plant and care for the trees, they uncovered their own strength, rooted their voices in the hallowed land. They learned how the degradation of the environment was connected to the degradation of their culture and communities, the deforestation of their own worth.

Half the world's children today live in severe, desperate deprivation, due to hunger, poverty, infection with HIV/AIDS, or caught in one of the ongoing thirty or so wars around the world.

Why are we not taking care of the children?

I am remembering where I was in 1977, a night sitting on my front porch of my 1906 carriage house in Berkeley. Just a cup of tea before turning to homework in Statistics, a sure sleep potion. I loved that porch, enough room for the whole family, friends and pets, and a view of anybody walking down the street, a Midwestern neighborly welcoming porch. I had finally put Jeremy, four, and Susannah, two, to bed. He wanted to hear "Where the Wild Things Are" again, and again. Zanna had many songs to sing about her day, the yellow finches in their cage, lonely, how Raggedy Ann was looking for Raggedy Andy, forlorn, how she herself was hungry and not at all tired and wondering if her rabbit George II is cold in his cage and could he maybe come sleep with her?

Weeks later Jeremy was crying at 10:30 at night,

"Mommy I can't sleep, Susannah is singing again!"

So I moved her into the bedroom at the front of the house where I kept my sewing stuff, dragging her rocking horse, all the stuffed animals, Babar and bears, a pink mother pig with three babies attached with shiny silver snaps, a huge huggable black whale, pillows covered in red and white Marimekko fabric. The only things I could sew were square or rectangular. Well, that sleeping arrangement lasted exactly one night. Not a full night. At 8pm, my exhausted but sleepless on-the-go boy called,

"Mommy! I can't sleep without Susannah singing."

So back she went. I could hear her singing softly in the background. He was totally conked out.

What was I doing back then? Some nights I was so tired with school, working, the kids, I'd try to sneak a nap while they were watching Sesame Street or Mr. Rogers. One day after my catnap slid into one a little longer, I came into the living room to find a new world, constructed by the thinking collective of their two and four year old selves. They had taken every one of the spools of thread out of my plastic turquoise and white flowered sewing kit and had stretched thread from one end of the living room to the other. Spooling around the furniture over the lamps as high as they could reach, or climb, and into the dining room. A dense and masterful web of every imaginable color and varying textures. Embracing every bit of solid matter and binding it all together with their attention, their passion. Stringing lines of magic, unbound hearts, unlimited imaginings to make a home for happiness. Rock-a-Bye thought she was in cat heaven, batting the lines and chasing dangling ends of thread. I left it up, our happy web, until it sagged to a natural death by the end of the week. We ate in the kitchen anyway, I wasn't doing a whole lot of formal dinner parties. It just felt more alive than our usual grand Berkeley carriage house, antiqued, trying to maintain its sense of conventional propriety and history. Thankfully, Mother didn't drop by in for a surprise visit.

That night, I fixed myself a cup of English Breakfast tea, with milk and honey, and went outside to sit on the brown wicker rocking chair. The pillow covered in a dark green paisley. It was so good to sit down. Grilled cheese sandwich dinner and dishes done, laundry humming away in the dryer, kids pooped and peaceful. I was looking at the eucalyptus trees across the road, the sky still deep blue with bunches of white clouds piled up, the faintest beginnings of the sun setting, pink and orange streaks stretched out behind the Claremont Hotel tower. All of a sudden, it got very still. The air went completely silent, as if something was going to happen or I had stepped into another world.

There was a circle above me in the clouds, but also around me. My dearest women friends were there, those alive and dead, women I don't know, my grandmother, my godmother, in a circle holding hands. They were all smiling, and dancing. A feeling of total rest peace and comfort in my small pinpoint of awareness grew to include all the trees, and the whole sky. I was at once immensely large at one with the sky and connected to all these women who I loved, who loved me, but at the same time I felt how very, very small I was, one of the molecules in the chair, the porch, the grass and the dirt. A speck in this infinite universe. This vision lasted for some time, while I experienced going back and forth almost at the same time between my infinite largeness and my microscopic littleness. How connected we all were, everything was. I wasn't alone. I knew my place in the world and the world's place in me. Then, slowly, the image, the feeling, faded and I was back in this chair, on the porch, drinking my tea.

I always thought having a spiritual experience was going to involve burning bushes, thunderclaps, or a deafening voice. But this was a day like any other, an ordinary day, a Tuesday evening, a simple cup of tea in my rocking chair. All this beauty. Miracles. Perhaps the sacred is just this ordinary, and common, and always there.

As I look at Wangari's picture, these long full years since 1977, I wonder if I have done all I'm meant to do, for this world, and for the children, mine, and that heart-wrenching half of the world's children. I am encouraged by Clarissa Estes:

> "The wild feminine is not only sustainable in all worlds, it sustains all worlds. Let us admit it. We women

are building a Motherland: Each with her own plot of soil eked from a night of dreams, a day of work. We are spreading this soil in larger and larger circles, slowly, slowly. One day it will be a continuous land, a resurrected land come back from the dead."

This is the time to shed our fears and give hope to one another so all our trees, 30 million and more, will bear fruit. We carry the seedlings of the future, including the children whose world this will be.

Herstory

"I know all about history.
But what about Herstory?"
- Susannah, age 6

Sitting on my deck over the water as the sun rises behind me, I watch the mountain, Mount Tamalpais, glow rose. Sunlight begins to shimmer on the water, sending white flames of light across the grey wooden railings and decks across the channel. A snowy egret squawks. The full moon is barely visible, suspended silken on a pale blue sky like a mirage. Dancing boat shadows white and cobalt blue. Ribbons of energy weave above and below between the seen and the unseen.

A lone duck paddles in the rippled water, pauses to look at a sunny yellow kayak floating. What is that? When it doesn't move, quack, honk or screech, she continues on her way, buoyant on barely visible sunny yellow feet.

I think of how we float like her, carried by our own personal stories, down the channels and rivers of our lives while much deeper, and in the dark, moves an older story.

A news story in the paper this morning describes the discovery of a new river, approximately two miles beneath the Amazon River, by a young female graduate student named Elizabeth Pimentel. It will be called Rio Hamza, for the supervising scientist. The deeper river appears to be as long as the Amazon, some 3,700 miles, but it is hundreds of times wider. It flows much slower.

Perhaps we are like that, too, with the deep, wide, slow river of our souls carrying the larger story.

Many years ago, I had this dream:

I am in a line of Native American women dressed in pale buckskin decorated with turquoise beads. We are walking down the path to the river from the forest. Next to the water, on the large flat granite river rocks, we unwrap our bundles, carefully placing their contents on the rocks. The sun is glistening off the water. I have waded out to a rock midway in the gently flowing river. Our task is to line up everything you have in your bundle with the lines of energy that come through the rock. These energy currents are very powerful and come from deep within the earth.

Everyone has everything they need in their bundle. The knowledge, the wisdom, unique gifts and talents, potential power. But these things must be lined up with the energy of the deeper source in order to be brought to life. We arrive in community, yet each woman has her particular place in the river, and a bundle only she carries. We have our own original medicine to bring back to the world. It also is important that we come as a community to the river, that we will all leave as keepers of the water, with our bundles now enlivened by her deep source of energy.

We are undergoing a shift in history, an evolution of consciousness, that only happens every 3,000 years.

Like Earth, Water is a female element. St. Francis called the river "Sister Water." The treasures of the deep river are the treasures of our own wild souls. This keeps us in the heart of things, sustains all life.

The divine Feminine is found in the earth, and in

openings to the earth: Lagoons, caves, lakes, wells, volcanoes, rivers. The meridians of the earth, here coming up through the rocks and river water, act like chakras, transporting energy and information. This dream river is a luminous river, one of the *rios de luz* that helps us find our own divine light.

The river shows us the way to align ourselves with our deeper purpose, and by doing so we have a limitless source of energy.

For us, in this time, it is the story of forgotten feminine wisdom and power, the mysteries of the dark, and lunar consciousness.

The task for women to claim their most authentic and effective power is to connect to deep wisdom and inner authority. As Clarissa Pinkola Estes says, "To be strong does not mean to sprout muscles and flex. It means meeting one's own numinosity without fleeing, actively living with the wild nature in one's own way."

What does *wild* mean? Among other definitions: passionately eager or enthusiastic; going beyond normal or conventional bounds; Fantastic! Sensational! Untamed, unbroken, mighty, strong.

The river beneath the river has come out of hiding, it has emerged. Stream forth, come up, arise, come into view. Begin, start, stick your neck out, spring forth. Rise from an obscure or inferior position or condition to come into being. The time is emergent. It calls for urgent action, arising as a natural, logical consequence of the history that has gone before, for thousands of years.

Come to the river, bring your bundle to life. The journey is spiritual in a feminine way. Not away from and out of the body or the Earth, toward the light of the sun and limited rational knowledge, but downward, and into our bodies, into the dark mysteries of our wild souls. Where wisdom, creativity, imagination abide.

As Rilke says,
"If we surrendered
to earth's intelligence
we could rise up rooted, like trees."

The pull of the soul is downward.

And so, in the dream, we return to the riverbank, bringing our bundles, now enlivened and full of power.

One of the meanings of indigenous is *born from within*. Also: immanent, deep-rooted inseparable, in the blood. This is where our wisdom, our true power abides.

Born from within. Here is the journey to a deepening of the soul going inward, down, in the directions of water and earth, towards the Feminine archetype and energies. Into our bodies and blood wisdom.

To call back our power is a reclamation project. This culture values the sun and the full light of day, ignoring the wisdom of the moon and darkness. Rational thought alone is narrow and sterile, whereas intuition brings up new possibilities. We need to see the fullness of our own souls, by staying close to darkness and all its mystery.

Bring the greening powers of the deep waters, the revivifying waters of the Feminine. Remember that the way of the river is not straight, and neither is your life course.

"I cannot believe that the inscrutable universe turns on an axis of suffering; surely the strange beauty of the world must somewhere rest on pure joy."

- Louise Bogan

Manta Ray

The alarm clock shocks me awake at 4:15am the morning of the lunar eclipse. It is too cold, too early, too dark. I burrow back into my white bamboo sheets, the shirred silken turquoise quilt. At 6am I am pulled out of bed, remembering sleepily this rare event. I grab my navy sweatsuit to put on over my grey 100% cotton DKNY pajamas. The full moon hangs over Mount Tamalpais, almost completely shadowed. I expected the moon to be black or grey, but like a thing alive it glows burnt sienna, then copper red. There are dark spots on the surface, nicks and scars. Craters where lost things fall into the dark deep and are forgotten forever.

I think of my mother.

Last winter she lay in her hospice bed, her body shriveled as memories bloomed. She told me she had always wanted to be an opera singer. The old college friend she had recently reconnected with was in truth her first love but her parents disapproved. They took her on a trip around the world for a year to break them up. Long ago, before my brother and sister died, she believed in God.

Although we came to a kind of peace those last illness laden years, she was still so angry at me she barely mentioned me in her will.

My private practice was drying up along with my own capacity for compassion. Stripped bare, emptied of faith, I was tired. I needed an adventure. I decided to return to Hawaii, to swim with wild dolphins, to wash away my losses in the warm ocean. Perhaps I could find a way to lure the sun back into my life.

In Kona just after dawn, I board the small white boat with a dark green canopy named *Uhane Nui O Nai'a*, "Great Spirit of the Dolphin" with nine other guests. Our native islander captain wears a navy blue, white hibiscus print Aloha shirt. His white cap reads "Sunlight on Water" in gold script.

As we head out of the harbor, Captain "China" Mike turns a large pink and white conch shell to the East, first, as he offers a prayer, *pule*, of praise and blessing the sea and all her creatures. In each of the four directions he blows a sonorous trumpet call, which resonates in my heartbone. Then the thirteen of us, crew and guests, join hands in a circle to breath together, to offer our thanks, to ask for protection.

The water sparkles as we lose sight of land, looking for dolphins. Captain spots a pod close to the shore, and soon they are swimming alongside our boat, surfing the wake at the bow in a fizz of bubbles. Ebullient, they spill into the air.

A dolphin stretches out of the water, sprung from gravity into the sky as pure joy. Slender nose to the sky, gold sun flecks along her muscular back, she twirls once, twice, an impossible seven times, somehow standing, a dancer in *jete*. Her black tail froths the surface as she turns. In pairs, they soar, frolic, vault out of the waves, bubbling up from the sea in a steady stream of jubilance. Leading the way along the bow of the boat, every few seconds one breaks away, unable to contain herself. She leaps straight up and hangs suspended. Another vaults head over tail, returns to the water with a resounding slap: "Ta Da!" One arcs so high we can see the community of dozens making their foamy way forward.

The boat stops just ahead of a large pod. We dive into the water to greet them. Dozens, maybe a hundred dolphins are packed to my right. I lie on my side, arms behind my back, aligning myself with them, waving my flippers. Their foreheads fold to make a slight ledge over their eyes, curve over the long, slender beak, black at the tip. Three-toned dark grey along their top, a light grey band in the middle, their bellies white, slightly pinkish. Each sleek section elegantly delineated, manicured, well groomed. Such formal dress for such a rambunctious lot.

Underwater, light flickers along their flanks. Eventually, it seems the light emanates from within. They undulate smoothly, their beaks straight ahead, just the slightest arc of their backs and strong tail propelling them, making a joke out of the long hours I spent in the high school lap pool practicing "the dolphin kick." Even pilgrimage can be full of frolic, play, and joy.

Pairs in the pod swim touching one another, caressing. A mother and baby swim just below me, the baby circling above and below her mother, poking her in the side with each revolution. My ears hum, not quite a ringing. Perhaps it's the murmur of the current over the sand, whispering secrets. A low chirping, like purring, comes from the crowd of dolphins to my right, although not a one comes over to nod and squeak at me. I am content to have them not move away, to let me swim alongside, only glancing at me now and then calmly.

The ocean sways and rocks us gently - seaweed, fish, dolphins, millions of invisible small lives. A school of black tang fish, each outlined in neon turquoise with yellow tabs at their tails, envelopes me as one of them. We travel for our own reasons, but are together swinging in the same peaceful rhythm of a great soothing heartbeat.

Time slips away. I could follow the dolphins forever. But no matter how hard I kick, they are pulling away. When I come to the surface I do not see the boat or the other swimmers for several breathless moments. Water slurps in my snorkel as I wonder if I have been left behind. Not by our stalwart captain and crew. I can trust them.

Although I had made a reservation for the nighttime swim with manta rays the same day as the swim with the dolphins, as we head back to the harbor in the afternoon I am beginning to question my decision. It's going to be pitch black. Weren't manta rays known as "devil fish"? And remember the tragic end of poor Steve

Irwin, pierced in his heart by a sting ray. I had to hear for the tenth time that manta rays are not the ones with stingers. Gabe, one of two crew members, was ecstatic about the rays. "Dude, they're fantastic! You won't believe it!"

It's a once in a lifetime experience, I reminded myself. The crew is well prepared and knowledgeable. None of the guests on our boat asks about sharks. I concentrate on not thinking about them.

This will be a very different adventure.

We headed to Keauhou Bay where the rays were spotted yesterday.

As the sun sets, the horizon blazes orange and pink, then thins into lavender threads. I look over at the pile of black wetsuits the crew is beginning to distribute. Four months ago, the tour company questionnaire had me fill in my weight to reserve a wetsuit. At that time I weighed 170 pounds, but figured four months was a long time away. Surely I could lose fifteen pounds before I spent a week on the beach in my bathing suit. I entered "155 pounds" as my weight. Now, I realized, at 172 pounds, I would need a larger wetsuit.

"Do you have any bigger sizes?" I asked hopefully.

The twenty-year-old surfer fit crew woman Krista

frowned.

"We brought only one suit for each person. Didn't you get the size you asked for?"

I nodded, shrugged. This was probably not going to work. Maybe I would miss the plunge after all. My eyes stung with regret.

Two of the women guests, overhearing our conversation, came over to help. Lips pursed, feet planted firmly on the deck, they vigorously pushed and pulled the rubbery skin over me until I was firmly encased, zipped, and still breathing.

One by one, we slid off the rear boat platform into the chilly black water with our snorkels and masks. We clutched little glow sticks like the ones they use at raves. I carried a small flashlight for me and my swimming buddy. Ten of us hung on to a flotation ring, flat and face down, keeping our flippered feet stretched out flat on the water's surface to not get in the way. I follow instructions, although I am sure no manta would swim that close. Divers on the ocean floor twenty feet below turn on their floodlights to fool the plankton into their normal daytime swirling, foaming clouds of manta ray food.

After half an hour, we are getting cold and wonder if this is another night of no sightings, as the previous night had been for the crew. We hang out for more than half an hour, silent. I'm cold and soggy squishy in my rubber skin. It could not be any blacker, the line dissolved between sky and sea. Then, a shadow dances along the sandy floor. We snuffle a collective "Ah!" as the dark wings lift through the murky water. Eight feet across, she rises scooping the bountiful plankton into her mouth with the two unfurled cephalic lobes on either side of her mouth. Each time she rises, she loops over on her back, circling us, inches away. A second, smaller manta, a mere six feet across, joins her. We later find out it is her sister, named Elsa.

Their silvery white undersides look like velvet, striped with gills. We swimmers hum into our masks at each pass, our flippers flat and motionless, as the two mantas swoop, loop, then glide away.

As she comes to the surface, where we hang suspended, she delicately turns over with ballerina grace, and circles her soft speckled belly, striped with gills, inches from my own. Belly to belly, I can almost touch her skin. I feel her huge gentleness, her wish to be close to us, to pass on her medicine, her wisdom.

She is so magical, so gentle, I imagine what it would be like to have her wrap her wings around me, like a mantle, like an angel, like the wise old unbelievable creature she is.

My mask is foggy with tears.

We are used to seeing angels as arriving from the bluest of sunny skies, on fluffy white clouds, bringing light and ease. Maybe angels also come from darkness, from the deepest unknown, looking strange and scary but bringing blessings nonetheless. The way life opens up sometimes in unfathomable darkness surprises us with new beauty. Magic. And grace.

Black Madonna:

An Expanding Universe Story

It is early spring, cool and windy, as I drive up Highway One along the Sonoma Coast. Deep purple iris peep out from a tangle of upstanding green grasses. Clumps of orange poppies merrily bounce in the wake of passing motorists. Carpets of yellow wild mustard and pale blue flax soften the rocky slopes. Arriving at my destination, the cliffside Timber Cove Inn, I begin to sink into the symphony of the crashing sea, the whistling wind. On a cliffside terrace, gray rocks splashed with burnt sienna lichen shelter a tangled bed of sea pink flowers. Inside, there is a huge stone fireplace inside, massive walls, cathedral windows to the sea, the poles and beams of redwood and Douglas fir. This is a powerful place where you can feel, listening with your skin, the right relationship between the wild outside and the wild soul inside, the true rhythms of our own nature.

I used to come here for weekend respites, decades ago, when the children were little. This trip is a little bit nostalgia, and a lot more curiosity about the Madonna sculptures in the Bay Area created by Beniamo Bufano. For decades there was a Black Madonna statue to greet visitors at the San Francisco Airport. Made of steel and black granite, the twenty-seven foot "Mother of All Nations" enfolded a four-eyed mosaic child. It was moved to make room for a parking lot. This Bufano statue is still here, standing ninety-three feet tall on a small rocky hill that reminds me of Irish burial mounds. A large open hand of redwood with a gold palm rises from her concrete and lead body. On both sides, a mosaic child encircled. The sculpture's name is Madonna of Peace, also called "The Expanding Universe."

What if we expanded our view of God to include her, the child, and the wild place in which she lives? What if we remembered, by sensing with our hearts, the time when the earth was believed to be female, and sacred?

The Catholic Church has a new Pope who taken the name of St. Francis. Like much of the world, I watched for the announcement, the white smoke of burning ballots from the Vatican chimney that would inform us that the College of Cardinals had made their decision. Wondering why there could not be a single church woman as part of this decision. A woman priest. Priests who could marry. Priests who do not abuse children. Perhaps the new Pope, an Argentinian who seems to be a man of the people, humble, accessible, will bring the love and respect for all creatures, including his sisters in the Church, that St. Francis of Assissi had.

I wonder what kind of a church it would be that included the leadership of women. A Church leadership that listened to wise and powerful nuns of the Leadership Conference of Women Religious in the United States who represent 90% of American nuns. Like nuns everywhere, they provide compassionate and generous care to the poor, the homeless. They educate the students, tend to the patients. Like women everywhere, they do the daily demanding tasks of care for children and families. But according to the older white male hierarchy of the Church, the nuns are too silent on matters of importance, like the condemnation of homosexuality, or the fervent defense of no contraception and no abortion.

The nuns have been scolded for their inclusive acceptance of all people, especially the most in need, which seems pretty God-friendly to me. Scolded in a Vatican assessment for "pushing radical feminist themes incompatible with the Catholic faith," the nuns continue to do their work, to engage in dialogue, to act with inclusiveness, to express their loyalty to their faith. To the essential authority of God. They continue to assert their devotion to the Church and to their mission, defined as "to give ourselves away in love, particularly to those in greatest need." What if we, the world, had a Church run by women?

Recently I visited Grace Cathedral for a woman friend's ordination as an Episcopalian priest. Near the entrance to the church, I passed Bufano's powerful black granite statue of St. Francis that stands in front of a pillar near the church entrance. It was a numinous experience to be given communion by a woman, a shock, like a small lightening bolt. Like the birth of a new universe.

Once I dreamed such a new beginning:

There is a little white clapboard church/schoolhouse on a small hill. The steeple has both a cross and a bell. There is a terrible splintering, groaning noise as the roof and timber collapse. In the middle of the room, a shriveled old white man with a long white beard disappears under the planks and plaster. Then, out of the settling dust strides a monumental black woman. She is dressed in ruby red satin, a turban around her head. And in her arms, also wrapped in red satin, is a baby girl.

In this darkening time, when all the old structures are dissolving, this time of chaos, the space is opening for new possibilities to emerge. Hidden in darkness is our own wholeness, restored one heart at a time. When the old lifeless economic and political structures and institutions have splintered and shattered and the narrow, sterile viewpoint of the single fearful old white man has shriveled, the Black Madonna steps out with new life. The color of earth, the color of regeneration, she redeems the world of matter by restoring the heart of care and the soul of meaning.

This Black Madonna is a feminine face of god that is

not only spirit, but matter. A vibrant figure who unites heaven and earth. Return us to the matter, the *mater*, of the earth, to being the humans we are meant to be. Of *humus*, of the earth. Humble. Make peace instead of making a killing.

As a symbol of an indigenous woman, she is "born from within." The red is celebratory. Wiseblood. Calling us to something new. A renaissance. A vision to awaken us to action. She invites us to our depths where we know better.

This image of the archetypal Dark Feminine brings "the blood knowledge, the green heart knowledge, the connection to the living streams of life" described by Andrew Harvey. The Black Madonna in my dream is African. Perhaps she speaks Zulu, where the greeting *Sawubona* (popularized in *Avatar*) literally means "we see you." Not *I* see you, but *we*. My eyes, connected to my ancestors, to the divine. We see each other and commit to our mutual potential for life and for freedom. When we have our eye on the connection and allow an openness to that person's highest good, we are actually doing what is most natural, most in line with scientific and spiritual truths.

The economic crisis is fundamentally a spiritual crisis. It is based on the underlying invisible but dominant myth of the dynamic masculine archetype, which functions from the illusion of separateness from each other, from nature, and fears losing, or being a loser, in a distorted either-or worldview.

But nothing in the universe exists independently. Even the smallest of structures is more open space than solid matter. And we, too, are indivisible from everything and everyone else. There is no such thing as a thing. No such thing as an individual. There is only the connection and process of the space in between, the indivisible relationship between everything in the universe. God, too, exists in the in-between and among us. The separate individual is a myth, an illusion, an obsolete old story and a very destructive one at that. We impact each other as the individual instruments in an orchestra influence each other. Like the music of a symphony or a jazz ensemble, the process is dynamic, always changing.

What can we call into being that is beautiful, harmonious, rich, peaceful?

These are disastrous times for many, homeless and hungry in this rich country. Around the world, half the world's children live in poverty, or preventable illness, or war zones. These are financially profitable times for the very few. Money has been mistaken for wealth. But the widespread chaos and dissolution of old forms also is making way for new freedoms, new possibilities. Here is the hidden goddess in matter, full of creative, dynamic energy. We need to cultivate her fierce compassion, her dynamic, creative energies, her concern for future generations.

As an archetype, both an image and an energy, the Black Madonna is available to us all. From the deep earth, fertile with life, she emerges out of darkness where all possibilities are born. Bringing new vitality, care, connection, creativity. Available and accessible, no longer in exile, without liturgy or curriculum, prayer book or priest. The power of a mother's heart, for all those who care for the earth and her children. A sheltering presence for new life. We seek wholeness. We have to see what is ill and unbalanced to change it. John Archibald Wheeler says,

> "We are participators in bringing into being not only the near and here, but the far away and long ago."

The time is now to bring the fierce compassion, the soul force, and authority of the sacred feminine back to the world. In the wisdom of our own hearts, we are pulled down to the earth, to our nature, and away from the scorching light of numbers that have no meaning, separated from what truly matters. Without our connection to our own wild souls, we are not quite human.

"The knowledge of the heart is in no book and is not to be found in the mouth of any teacher, but grows up out of you like the green seed from the dark earth."

- C.G. Jung, *The Red Book*

Shooting Star: A Letter to Janet

April 1, 2004

Dear Janet,

Wow! You're a grandmother. No fooling. I just got a letter from Link with a delightful picture of laughing fellow Emmett James Graham Bertram. That's a solid grounded Midwestern name from your wild girl child, now mother. Sounds like the beginning of a country song, or long poem. "Emmett James Graham Bertram set off for the river one day. Looking for fish, running from sorrow, hoping his darling would stay." He looks like Amanda with those fat dimpled cheeks and twinkling eyes. But blue not mahogany brown. Uncle Nick calls him M-It. I last saw Nicky when his sturdy brave little 8 year old self dedicated his soccer game to your memory. They won.

Amanda gave birth in Swedish Hospital, the East Wing, where you labored to accept death with grace and open hands, 18 years ago to the day. I'm sure you were there again, cheering her on, protecting her. You must be so proud. The wheel turns again.

When my Jeremy was being born, two months before Amanda, you walked your abundant self up three flights of stairs to leave crepes in the fridge. Three different kinds of filling: Dungeness crab, creamed spinach, and one with chicken and mushroom. I was so happy there was good food to eat when I got home from Alta Bates Hospital. So moved by your thoughtfulness, I cried. Well maybe it was also that I was exhausted, scared, carrying this no longer quite so mysterious little bundle of gold, to a bed where the cat had peed in immediate resentment. The winter storm had blown in through the French doors that Steve had to break when he locked himself out of the house without the car keys in the rush to get to the hospital. I have a picture of Amanda and Jeremy a few months later, naked on your white shaggy rug, Amanda staring adoringly at this joyful baby trying to poke her eye. We kept that rug for a long time after you and Link moved up to Seattle, and we moved in.

It was a Tuesday morning in September. I was going to fly up to Seattle Friday; finally you had a free weekend, or were ready to let me see you post chemotherapy, bald. We hadn't talked since Sunday, and I woke up with a cold heavy sense of dread weighing me down like a metal cape, making it hard to breathe. I tried to reach you by phone, but your guy Tom said No, you weren't there, but you were fine. It's just that you had a sore throat and they wanted to check you out at the hospital. My voice screeched upward, and he got correspondingly calm, reassuring. He would be there in a few hours to bring you lunch. "No now, now you have to go NOW!" I kept screaming. An hour later, sitting in my green overstuffed armchair across from a young woman patient, a streak of white yellow light shot horizontally across the darkened room. A jolt went through my body and I thought "She's gone."

Tommy called me at home before noon. The sound of his voice cracked my heart, an iceberg floated off the shore of a glacial land mass. I sat down hard on the floor. He said he had gone immediately that morning to see you.

When he walked in the hospital West Wing room you were sitting on the bed in Lotus position, palms open, with your back to the door. You said "Don't talk" and continued with your breathing, your trying to breathe, still, silent, centered. When your bald head and your hands began to turn blue, Tommy ran into the corridor to get help. They called a Code Red or is it Blue, and jumped on you with all their skill and equipment. You were already leaving.

Do you remember that summer we sat out in Suzy's hot tub to watch the meteor shower? After hours we came in and held hands in our sleeping bags, next to each other. It took me a long time to fall asleep that night. My mind was unbound, and flashing a series of visions. The stream of images moved fluidly from one form to another, all related, everchanging, different versions of the myriad forms of things in the world. In vivid colors, from one object to another, it was like a series of slides or movie frames but smoother, not choppy, gliding from one form to another. In slow motion each object transformed continually, maybe infinitely, from one thing to another. A candlestick and all the varieties of sizes and colors and shapes of candlesticks became a pencil and all the sizes and shapes of that and then table legs and trees and flowers of every shape and color, rose buds and dying roses, and hats and every thing you could think of, natural and manmade. In this series it was so clear, so beautiful, to see that they were all related. It made perfect sense how each became the other, all the same changing energy and yet different too. Forms that were unique and separate and still for at least a moment. Lasting a second or a lifetime.

I missed the magic that came with you, the faith, the fun I had in my life when you were alive. A few years later I took the kids up to the UC summer camp, Lair of the Bear, Camp Gold of course, never Camp Blue, where we usually went for a week. Camping with beds, all meals prepared, adults to talk to and a day's worth of fun wear-the-child-out group activities with child care for the youngest. Did I mention single mother cheap? I was in such a funk that summer, tired, depressed and banking zero in my trust in God account. All I want to say about my boyfriend of that time is that he was a trained nurse and carpenter, loved sex, and at age 48 still rode a bike. He wasn't too interested in being a grown up, either working or parenting, so here I was with the kids, alone again.

After campfire, a visiting astronomer set up his high powered telescope for us to look at stars from the meadow. Waiting in line, looking at this huge dome of darkness with little pinpricks of light, which pretty much matched the proportions of my black mood, I did a silent prayer. Started a conversation with God. Actually it was more on the demand-command side of things than the plea for mercy or gratitude for existence. I challenged you first, old buddy, to show your face. Where are you? Why did you leave? Not that you could help it. The one responsible for this mess of loss was God, who was really failing me. I threw my defiance like a spear up as far as I could. I don't believe in you anymore. You're not helping. I'm exhausted, lonely, broke, and tired of struggling. If you really exist, show me a sign. Otherwise...I'm not sure what I was thinking there, some kind of a continuing strike, boycott. Looking up, nothing was happening. Silence.

"OK God," I say, generously giving him, her, another chance. And then, bringing out a ploy from my limited reservoir of patient mothering responses, "I'm going to count to 10." I began slowly, sternly, 10 - 9 - 8. Right about then, I heard myself, my little pinprick self under this vast dark dome sparkling with stars, asking God to prove himself. I got it, the absurdity of it. I breathed, said "Ah", and something shifted in my chest, cracked. I felt it, heard it, a little whispered "click" like the sound-feeling when my bag of waters broke, click, announcing Jeremy's descent beginning and I let go.

Opened as wide as I could, and surrendered. Somewhere between "8" and "7" a shooting star streaked across the sky, splitting the darkness with a lifeline of love.

Falling in Love with Ilya

This morning, in honor of my yearning for a tropical summer, I had a papaya. Glossy orange with a pink, sunrise blush and spirited green speckles. Such an easy bit of luxury and abundance. It reminds me of a dream I had thirty years ago:

On the hillside of the park a smiling old woman hands out luscious large papayas to anyone on the trail who wants one. There are couples strolling, young children skipping and riding bikes. Hikers stride with their wooden poles, dogs scamper happily. The grassy hill alongside the trail teems with *wildflowers, blossoming vines and fruit trees with gigantic fruit. As we walk, we gradually wind our way down to the valley floor and enter a rectangular building like a military barracks for a meal. There are long tables set with identical square white place mats and plates. Waiters dressed in black tuxedoes place slivers of papaya in the middle of each plate. Each individual portion costs $50.00. We look at each other and laugh at the absurdity.*

This dream showed the contrasts between a natural world of abundance, the domain of the wild feminine, and the military precision and black and white thinking of the static masculine mind, where what was available to all becomes rigidly controlled and distributed for the good of the few.

When I had this dream, I had just begun graduate school. I was fiery with my desire to place women at the center of her own story, her own psychology. And I had fallen in love with Ilya.

He was the unlikeliest of loves: A Nobel prize winning chemist, in contrast to my very nearly not-graduating from UC Berkeley because of my science grade. Also he was married, and someone I would never meet. Perhaps it is more accurate to say I fell in love with his mind, his theory of dissipative structures, and the hope it offered to reconcile our estrangement from the world. The images of the open, non-equilibrium systems in the Belousov-Zhabotinsky oscillations seemed beautifully feminine to me with their curved lines, elegant scrolls, rounded forms, and asymmetrical patterns.

In 1975, *Order Out of Chaos* appeared as "La Nouvelle Alliance" by Ilya Priogine and Isabelle Stengers. Ilya later won the Nobel Prize for his theory of dissipative structures, open and complex systems existing far from equilibrium which, after a period of turbulence, perturbation and chaos, suddenly leap into new more inclusive and complex patterns of order, much like the shifts of a kaleidoscope. Chaos itself becomes a creative source of new order.

Ilya was introduced to me by author and revolutionary networker Marilyn Ferguson in her newsletter *Brain/Mind Bulletin.* His discoveries and poetic philosophy inspired me to return to graduate school for a PhD, to see what I could make of a woman-centered psychology of self that was grounded in both new science and the spiritual depth psychology of Jung. His ideas and the images resonated deeply with how my life, and the lives of women I knew, moved through so many changes and transformations.

In the new sciences of systems, chaos, complexity and emerging evolutionary theories in biology, there are many correspondences with Jung's model of the psyche as an open, self-organizing system. Women's lives could not be squeezed into the prevalent adult developmental models of age-related stages or stepladder changes. The depth and breadth of women's lives went way beyond the narrow definitions of relational helpful spouse or nurturing mother. Beyond her roles as muse, *inspiratrice*, Special Woman, or helpmate, a woman is the subject of her own life and development. Which as I well knew, involves chaos, turbulence, oscillations, synchronicities and leaps into new patterns, new order, new lives, from time to time. Ilya understood. And so did Jung, mostly.

The sciences of life and of the mind have been curiously at odds. In the worlds of biology and botany, scientists assume complexity is always building up. For physicists, on the other hand, it was accepted that everything in the universe runs down, to a state of inertia or entropy: a stagnant, dead, homogenous state. Our psychological models of the self and mind followed these explanations in classical science.

In large and complex systems like our own psyches, there are many available possibilities or degrees of freedom. This inevitably results in fluctuations, a kind of dynamic equilibrium. In certain cases, small fluctuations are amplified, driving the system to a new phase. A chance comment, a startling event, a synchronistic meeting, can change our lives forever.

It's striking that non-equilibrium is a source of order. When this occurs, the archetype of the dynamic, transformative feminine becomes visible. The law of entropy is often used as a measure of disorder, and a prediction of increasing disorganization and loss of useable energy. Applied to the aging process, this mindset scares us into thinking our vital and creative lives are over. Going downhill from here! But it is very possible that creativity and change are unlimited and continual.

In our lives, we experience times of conflict, crisis, situations or relationships that are stuck and cannot be resolved in a known way, a familiar way, or a reasoned way. When the oscillations are powerful enough, we reach a singular moment, a bifurcation point, and shift into a new order of being. Through this irreversible, creative process, we develop new rules of transformation. There is no going back. Every cell in our bodies is changed, simultaneously and immediately in the blink of an eye. This is not a linear path, nor does it depend on the slow structural building up of cumulative small laborious steps.

We change, grow and develop in a series of complexly organized constellations that succeed each other in surprising and unpredictable ways. Yet the new patterns of order are lawful and purposeful, according to the laws of our own nature, the self-organizing impetus of our souls. Chaos becomes something not to be feared, but a source of creativity and a new order.

This is why the linear lifespan approach to age and a step-by-step ladder approach are so incomplete for truly understanding women's lives. Or anyone's life. The tasks and challenges we are working on at any time exist on multiple levels, and are interdependent. Working on one of them works on all of them. When we go through periods of turbulence, chaos, indecision and uncertainty, if we are open and willing, cultivating the ears of our hearts, the eyes of our spirit, we transform ourselves. Often the leap into a new pattern, the shift in our consciousness, is precipitated by the smallest of events.

**

Women's ego identity begins in a related way, as a self-and-other. From this core, empathy and both/and thinking are natural and skillfully developed for the rest of our lives. We are aligned with the spiritual and scientific truths of interconnection and interdependence. Over many years of working with patients, the correspondences among new science, spirituality and the archetypal feminine became more and more clear. My life, and those of my colleagues and patients, seemed to unfold, to jump in a discontinuous way, a kind of "punctuated equilibrium" from one state to another, one integrated pattern of identity to the next. There were periods of turbulence, conflict, chaos, and then some small incident or thought or experience would catalyze a dramatic shift that changed everything.

> "Man's new dialogue with nature emphasizes that chaos represents not just hitherto unrecognized phenomena but an unjustly neglected set of values."
>
> - Ilya Prigogine

Chaos and the imagistic right side of the brain were long associated with – and disregarded alongside - women and the feminine. Women and the characteristics associated with them were considered inferior to the alternative, and evil.

In contrast to the Western view of chaos as evil, the

Taoists characterize chaos "*Hun-tun*" as generous, rich in possibilities. In many ways, the science of complexity speaks with the authority and voice of the Feminine. It focuses on certain attributes, energies, processes that have been dismissed, neglected, devalued.

Two decades ago, a physicist at Princeton said: "In science, the left hand is chaos, the right hand is order. If we are to get anywhere, we will have to integrate the two." The journey to wholeness is a weaving path, full of "fateful detours and wrong turnings." In this weaving path, we follow an unfolding, dynamic, transformative way. It is a creative process.

One of my dreams shows how this might look:

I am riding on a train overlooking deep green pastures, indigo mountains in the distance. There are four wild Appaloosas running around playfully in the grass. As I enjoy watching them, I am startled to realize the train tracks are not level. In fact, they are on wooden platforms that move in four directions while also moving forward. The levels move up and down, too. Not as steeply as a roller coaster but in a similar design. It is a very fluid way to travel. Flexible. Multidimensional. Travelling the four directions, including the four elements, up and down.

As the tracks move, it is like the shifting tides. I think: This would hold up even in the great energies of earthquakes.

When I woke up I thought: WomanTracks. This is how we travel. We can live in harmony with earthquakes. Like the Appaloosa, we are intelligent, sure-footed. We have endurance. We have stamina. We want to play.

Letting go of an outworn career, relationship, home, or way of being in the world, is never easy. It is a kind of death. And yet, without the letting go, the dying of the old, we do not have space, inside or out, for the new to emerge. As this happens in our individual lives, so it happens in our culture, and in the cultures of the world. *Enantiodromia* refers to the ancient idea that everything eventually turns into its opposite to restore balance. We are in the process of restoring balance as the archetypal Feminine - dynamic, transformative, creative - returns from exile to new science, to art, to every field and every endeavor.

The essential buoy to hold onto is the knowledge that life doesn't just "happen" to us. We participate in a significant way, at a soul level, with the creation of the new, ourselves and our world.

"A feminine [life] starts on all sides at once. Starts twenty times, thirty times over. There is a capacity to let go as well as to hold on."

- Helene Cixous

In 2007, after twenty-five years in private practice, I was beginning to get restless, feeling crowded and cloistered. Although I was very attached to my patients, and they were healing, lives transforming, I missed being more in the world. One warm summer evening, as I was leaving my second story office at sunset, I noticed an iridescent green hummingbird trapped in the rafters of the stairwell, crashing against the second story window in her desperation to get outside.

Although I worried that I would increase her stress dangerously by interfering, I had to get her out. I borrowed a broom from the florist downstairs, and spent the next half hour very slowly, over and over again, coaxing her down the length of the window until she finally ducked under the door overhang and flew into the scented summer evening. Down and out. A few weeks later the same thing happened. Was it the same or a different hummingbird? Thankfully, again, I was successful in helping her to find her way out. In all my years in this office, this had never happened before. It got my attention, in the way synchronicities do: something so striking, surprising, out of the ordinary and not easily explained, not logical. Yet it struck a deep chord of truth in me, right in the heart-bone. What did the hummingbird have to teach me?

Hummingbirds have huge hearts, the largest of any species in the world relative to body size. In flight, the heart beats 20 times a second. Very skillful flyers, they can fly backwards, forwards, sideways, or hover with their wings moving in a figure of eight, the symbol of infinity. Birds of great courage and perseverance, they can migrate thousands of miles. They are fiery fighters in protecting their territory. They communicate by dancing. They are often depicted as birds of resurrection, since they fall into torpor over night, slowing their fast 500 beats a minute hearts down to as low as 36, and then revive for a new day.

In some Native American religions, the hummingbird is a messenger between worlds. As such, they help shamans keep nature and spirit in balance. They are symbols for accomplishing that which seems impossible: for following joy, or believing in magic. They seem to do so many miraculous things.

It seemed unthinkable that I could, or would, leave a profession that had been the fulfillment of a long held dream at another time. And yet, this was the beginning of the death of my practice. It would be a while before I found my way through the portal into more beauty and joy.

"The way to the goal [individuation] seems chaotic and interminable at first and only gradually do the signs increase that it is leading anywhere. The way is not straight but appears to go around in circles. More accurate knowledge has proved it to go in spirals."

- CG Jung

Classical physics emphasized stability and permanence. A psychology of self derived from this science emphasizes stability, and fears chaos. Yet from Ilya we learn: The more degrees of freedom for self-organization, the more order and creative new patterns will emerge.

As human beings we are encouraged, prodded, pushed and pulled into our evolution as more expanded, inclusive, complex versions of ourselves. The goal is to become complete and whole. . . not perfect. In a popular quotation from poet Muriel Rukeyser: "The universe is made of stories, not atoms." But we now know a story about atoms: they are 99% open space, both wave and particle. They exist mainly as possibility and potential.

Great science and great art rest on the same foundations. Niels Bohr said this about atoms: "When it comes to atoms, language can be used only as in poetry. The poet, too, is not nearly as concerned with describing facts as with creating images."

We relinquish the certainty of classical physics for the indeterminacy, the unpredictability, of the mystery of life. We are not clocks, of course. We are not even crystals, for we are not symmetrical. We are not solid structures. This science, quantum theory, is the voice of the Feminine.

The language of hierarchy speaks to dominance and control. In contrast, the language of complexity theory speaks of organization created by attractors. In Jung's language of depth psychology, these organizing energies are known as archetypes. They are both self-organizing and self-transcending images and energies, unique to each one of us as we move towards becoming our whole, authentic selves.

Rather than the linear, sequential, cumulative picture of change according to the perspective of the archetypal Masculine, the Feminine description of change shows us circumambulating around a center, moving like a spiral to expansively and extravagantly include more and more multiplicity, richness, complexity.

Kathe Kollwitz
by Muriel Rukeyser

"Women as gates, saying:
The process is after all like music,
like development of a piece of music.
The fugues come back and
  again and again
interweave.
A theme may seem to have been put aside,
but it keeps returning--
The same thing modulated,
somewhat changed in form
Usually richer,
And it is very good that this is so."

Like a kaleidoscope, when a change occurs in one part of the round, the entire circle, the whole system, is changed. Just like the first stage of the alchemical process, old forms are broken down. It is a stage full of conflict, chaos, and turbulence. Yet within this pregnant darkness lie creative new possibilities.

It is not only a new pattern that is formed. In this transcendence, the rules for changing have also evolved. Each reordering produces greater complexity and a greater likelihood of change in the future.

Having explained his dissipative structures, Ilya took a major step towards healing the breach between the life and the nonlife sciences, granting humankind more control over our fate that ever imagined, and restoring our relationship with nature:

"We have the technology to make deserts flourish again. And now we know that we are not merely prisoners of circumstances. We know we can interact with nature. This is the heart of the message I give. Matter is not inert. It is alive and active...With the old idea of a doomed determinist world now gone, we can feel free to make our fate for good or ill. Nature is part of us, as we are part of it."

Observer and observed are indivisible, dancing each other into being. An ecological view, a holistic view, is based on the interdependence of all phenomena, the interdependence of all of us on this planet. The universe is a web of relationships. It is intrinsically dynamic. The transformative Feminine is the missing piece for our wholeness, and the catalyst for a new story.

What is emerging is a reconciliation of the Feminine with the Masculine, the scientist with the shaman, the priestess with the physician.

**

We are always participating in the co-creation of our world. Reality includes multiple truths, not opposing dualities. The propensity for either/or thinking is based on the linear logic of the Masculine, whereas the Feminine intelligence is an integrated, contextual, both/and way of knowing. A Feminine consciousness, whether awakened in women or men, takes the long view. It remembers that we are all part of a living universe.

We need trust to follow our intuition, to know that while we are seeking our future, our future is also seeking us. We learn to respond to resonance, to pay attention to what gives energy, to open to hunches, images, dreams that offer clues on how to proceed. To value the process, and accept that we are in partnership with the mystery, creator and created. We are not at war with nature when we are in alignment with our own natures.

Cooperation and harmony are ways of the Feminine. The void or chaos is the starting point for nearly all the world's creation myths.

Likewise, Ilya's idea of a creative void of chaos as a generative source of new possibilities corresponds to Jung's descriptions of the creative potential of the collective unconscious. Just as patterns emerge from the nonlinear dynamics of complexity theory, intuition and experiences of synchronicity arise to show us previously invisible patterns that connect inner meaning with outside reality, letting us know we are on our path.

Just as we can see the clouds but not the energies that move and change the clouds, so does an implicate order and energy unfold into visible, temporal, material structures, the explicate order. The hologram suggests a new understanding of the universe and our place in it, in which information about the whole is enfolded into each part, and the whole is more than a sum of its parts.

In the mechanistic view of classical science, parts are only externally related to each other, as if matter is separate from energy. But David Bohm shows us the internal relatedness of all the parts. This echoes Jung's understanding as well, and the wisdom traditions of indigenous tribes, of the predecessor to modern science-alchemy.

In relating his interpretation of quantum theory to

the origin of the universe, Bohm says:

"Imagine an infinite sea of energy filling empty space, with waves moving around us there, occasionally coming together and producing an intense pulse. . . To us, that pulse looks like a big bang; in the greater context, it's a little ripple. Everything emerges by unfoldment from the holomovement, then enfolds back into the implicate order. I call the enfolding process "implicating", and the unfolding "explicating." The implicate and explicate together are a flowing, undivided wholeness. Every part of the universe is related to every other part in different degrees."

We humans, like other material and spiritual beings, are like small ripples on an enormous ocean of energy, having only some relative stability in becoming manifest.

When we realize matter and consciousness are different aspects of everything in the universe, we include facts, meaning, and value equally in our definitions of self. When we integrate women's experiences and the archetype of the feminine, we have a new model of the self. An ecology of self.

Bohm continues:

> "If we can obtain an intuitive and imaginative feeling of the whole world as constituting an implicate order that is also enfolded in us, we will sense ourselves to be one with this world."

At some point in our lives, midlife, or older, we must ask *what have I contributed*? How does it benefit the world and the planet? Why did I come to life? This energy carries the new story. Through the dissolution of old forms and the emerging of new ones, we look for the patterns that connect.

This is a time of transition for the world. Most of us feel it. Some are so frightened by the changes, the dissolving of the old order, they are holding on for dear life to structures, practices, beliefs that do not foster life.

With the understanding of new science, we see that this universe is not static and closed, but is emerging, expanding, birthing. We are the midwives of a new world seeking to be born. We are the parents, the pilgrims, the pioneers, the priestesses and shamans, the physicians and scientists. We are the awakened dreamers and storytellers, each of us with a spark of the Divine. As Teilhard de Chardin described, there is a planetary web of evolving consciousness, a web of light to which we each contribute. At every moment, we are like holograms, both part of the whole and reflecting the whole. Together, we are more than the sum of our parts, bringing new possibilities into reality. What are we contributing?

If we truly love what we are doing, we become light as a feather. We learn to transcend the contradictions of duality and renew our joy in the magic of living.

The world is hungry for a vision. Now is the time for all the awakened dreamers to show us what they see, what they know. Now is the time for you to know that all you do is sacred. This is the path to renewal. It is time to reunite the masculine with the feminine, our material selves with our spiritual essence. To dance together, to dive down into joy.

"In all these developments, there was an element of surprise. Things that were impossible a few years ago seem to be possible today. And there is really the feeling that we live in this world of innovation, creativity, that we are...perhaps at a turning point."

- Ilya Prigogine

Uncharted Waters

"Everything you see has its roots
in the unseen world."
- Rumi

The week before Thanksgiving in 2009, I sat in my car at a stoplight after a yoga class, considering the imminent loss of my home. For a year, the bank who had taken over my loan sent me certified, "Intent to Foreclose" notices, after I let my mortgage payments get two months behind as recommended by a bank representative in order to qualify me for a loan modification. Two intensive loan modification attempts went into the black hole of "lost" paperwork, silence and stalling, until finally an honest clerk asked me if I had any equity in my home. "Yes," I answered, estimating secretly an abundant $250,000 according to an appraisal in 2007.

"The bank will never approve your loan modification then," he responded.

After pulling rabbits out of hats for many last minute saves in the past, it was really time to let go. Washed up, washed away, an unexpected road opened. It was time to sell while I still had the option.

Out the car window, I watched a black crow tuck her wings and dive towards the street. Just in the nick of time, she would swoop straight up to the sky, stretch her wings, do it again. What was she doing? Then I noticed she had a berry in her beak. She would toss her head before she dove, throwing the berry up high, then catch it before it hit the ground. Playing with the moment. I would need to feel my way into the pause between berry and no berry, the in between of the inbreath and outbreath. Perhaps I could delight in living there, too. Moment by moment.

In order to show the house, the real estate agents strongly recommended I move out with everything, as quickly as possible to avoid the rainy winter lull in sales. After the garage sale, an intensive clean-up, and renting storage space, I squeezed two suitcases, journals and a box of books into my old BMW convertible. I moved into the unheated art studio of an old high school friend. Six weeks later, the house still unsold, I moved in with my son, his fiance, her daughter, and two large dogs who kept me company on my twin bed in the spare room. As my worldly life got smaller and smaller, a surprising stillness and peace expanded.

This was, in fact a dream coming true. A terrifying dream that I'd had four years before:

I am walking down the corridors of a hospital, then into a large ward where there are rows and rows of beds on either side of the aisle. Patients lie with broken bones, legs held up in traction, bandaged bloody heads, IV drips. A woman is being prepared for surgery. I keep walking without stopping at any of the beds, murmuring "Sorry, sorry, I can't stop." I have to ignore their cries and moans. As I pass through the ward into an intersecting hallway I see a large yellow EXIT sign on the door. I push down on the handle to walk out, but instead of a floor, or stairs, there is nothing. Nothing. I am hundreds of feet up on the threshold of open space and there is no way back. The skyline looks like an old European city with steeples and carved gargoyles in the cathedrals, buildings, palaces around me. I close my eyes in terror, praying to God to just kill me. This fear is unbearable. But when I open my eyes, not only am I still alive but there is a handsome dark haired man with a handle bar moustache hanging by his knees off of the metal, fold down fire escape. He has on bright red tights. He is a trapeze artist. And he smiles with his arms outstretched, telling me without words how to fling myself into his arms and flip over his shoulders to the ground. There seems to be no other choice, so I leap, somersault over his shoulders, jumping the last few feet between the bottom of the fire escape and the sidewalk with a triumphant "Ta Da!"

Leap. Fall into the mystery of life.

Thresholds are liminal spaces, an in-between of time and space, taking us to the outskirts of what we know, beyond the borders and boundaries of familiar ground. Stepping into this void acknowledges a dissolution of the old order, a turning upside down of your life. It is a profound dislocation, terrifying but also a sacred space that makes room for new energies to enter and transform. At times like this, recurring throughout life, we need every ounce of courage, every helpful ally, human, animal, spirit.

I had been poised on this threshold for a long time, stressed and struggling, too cloistered in my upstairs office, imprisoned by economic forces beyond my control, too introverted in my depth psychology work. My soul yearned for more freedom. Hungered for beauty, renewal, joy. For a life I would love that did not yet have a name.

How do you want to live?

The closest I could come to an answer was I wanted to feel at home in the world and to love my life. I would need to become indigenous, born from within, to find my natural wild self, my place of belonging. I decided, once the house sold, to travel to a place I'd never been before in hope of finding some clues to a life I'd never lived before. A wild country, a peaceful country, where I could be immersed in nature and wildlife. Maybe I could learn to trust my intuition again, and wake up my soul. A friend had told me about Costa Rica, the land of *pura vida*. A country which designates a greater percentage of its of its land to natural parks and wilderness reserves than any other country in the world, where there is no standing army and obsession with violence, where 38% of the legislature is women, perhaps I could feel at home.

As I read on a brochure: *La vida es una sola. Sumergete en ella. Vivela profundamente.* There is only one life. Dive into it. Live it deeply.

Cultivating courage, I went ziplining. Then birdwatching in Monteverde Cloud Forest. Aided by an attentive native guide, our small group spotted six magical and rare quetzals. Green and aquamarine feathers around a crimson breast. Their haunting one, two, three note songs soar to heaven, long turquoise tail feathers drape towards earth. Visiting a beach park the next day, we spot a three-toed sloth, only a few feet away in a palm tree next to the path. Draped over a palm frond, she sleeps. Considers. In her gentle, deliberate way, stretches out farther on the palm frond which in a synchronizing slowness, bends toward the ground. The sloth, her flowing gray brown mane tinged a faint from the algae that, slowly, grow there, is unconcerned. She is used to life lived upside down. I study the sloth.

The maps of my psyche and the possibilities for my life begin to unfurl like the rainforest canopy.

We travel to Tortueguero on a long, slow bus towards the most stunning experience of the trip. Once over the mountains to the Caribbean side of Costa Rica, the air softens and falls like a moist silken drape. Hibiscus openhearted in orange, coral, shocking pink. Orchid giants on six foot tall stems, a froth of lavender, violet, and white. It was over 100 degrees F. in the bus, and we are so relieved to move to the flat canal boat for the trip into Parque Nacional Tortuguero. Ribbons of water weave through the lagoons as we listen to the bellows of the howler monkeys, spot a river otter which follows us for awhile. Egrets and a striped tiger heron. A small turtle suns herself on a log lush with scarlet bromeliads. The periscope eyes of a caiman bulge from the river grasses. The air is damp and fertile with river mulch.

A banner strung across the river welcomes us, "Bienvenido" but it is the toucan with her green-blue-yellow-red beak and the rat-a-tat-tat of the woodpecker who welcome us in grander fashion to the magic of this place.

It is late April, too late to see the green turtles and the *arribada*, the mass nesting of thousands of olive Ridley turtles. The guides say most of the turtles have left. But part of my dream trip to Costa Rica is to see a turtle nesting. At 10 p.m. on our first night in the village, our guide tells us about the turtles, drawing in the sand of our lodge with his bare feet the different shapes, sizes, and behaviors of the species of sea turtles. I feel he is invoking them, the way ancient peoples used to sing the turtles in from the sea. We cannot use our flashlights, which disorient the turtles, but the guides have special red lights that do not disturb. I am asked to change out of my thin white T-shirt because it might reflect too much moonlight. In a hurry to start walking the beach, I slip on a waterproof hooded turquoise jacket over my jeans. We are to be quiet, to walk, fast, in double lines. Only if we see a turtle will we each pay the guide $20.

The black sea gleams with the pearl of a full moon. It is so humid and hot I am beginning to stream sweat into my eyes, glasses fogging. Then, a half mile down the beach, a red light blinks. Once, twice, then fast three times. A turtle is digging her nest. We break into a trot. There is a swearing from the two thirty year old men behind me. I am on a mission and surge forward. Then, unable to see, I trip into an old turtle nest and hit the ground hard. I am the oldest member of the group by 20 years, and if I had broken something… But I am okay, now coated in sweat and sand, and setting a pace for the group that repairs my pride. When we get there, the turtle is still digging and we keep our distance. It's a leatherback. Huge. Four and a half feet long, close to 1,000 pounds, the guide estimates she is 30 years old. She has a great rounded back with seven ridges, but no bony shell.

The leatherback's front flippers are expansive like a great bird, a third the size of her body, and she labors to dig a hole up to her shoulder. Then she begins to shovel the sand behind her, with round flippers that look like paddles. Smoothing. Shoveling and throwing the sand aside. The flippers flowing over each other in an alternating synchrony. She pats the egg chamber one last time. She begins to drop her eggs, deepen in a trance. We approach. The guide shines his red flashlight under her rear flippers so we can see the eggs drop, several at a time, the size of raquetballs, soft and rubbery without shells. She sighs. A tear slides out of her eye. I remember naturalist Carl Safina's words and look them up later that night:

"The leatherback is one of the few original sentient beings. That it is a kind of human is indicated by its propensity to shed tears."

She continues until 95 or 100 eggs are dropped. A glistening mound of possibilities. Then she lays some smaller eggs, which are not fertile, on top. The scientists do not know why, but I think she is doing what she can to protect the living eggs by planting imposter eggs for the raccoons, dogs, coyote, jaguar, seagull, human poachers. She then swivels her flat rear flippers, like sensitive paddles. First one then the other, overlapping. Pats down the surface, and scatters sand all around to disguise the nest. To be certain, she moves slowly down the beach a ways and makes a shallow pretend nest, again scattering sand. When she has done all she knows to do, she turns toward the sea. Dragging her self along the sand she makes deep furrows in the sand like a tractor. We, silent, move into a column alongside her, like a parade, salute her by doing our version of a turtle dance, hands crossed and alternating in front of our bellies, swaying. We call out softly, congratulations and blessings. "Well done, Mama!" "Safe travel, Mother!" Streaming our tears, our hopes for a future for her, the hatchlings, and for all our children.

In 35-40 days, when the hatchlings, *tortuguitas,* emerge, they find their way following the light, into the vast deep mystery of the sea. Their tribe has swum the seas of the earth for 200 million years. With a great deal of luck, some will find their way back to this nesting beach.

For nesting, the leatherbacks prefer ruggedly pounded shores, dynamic beaches, which these days means many will lose their nests to erosion. Because their beaches are not reliable, they spread out their eggs, 4 or 5 clutches of perhaps 100 eggs, in different nests. Eventually, the nesting females will find their way back to this beach, if they survive. The odds are not high. Perhaps they find the way back to this beach to nest by the signature sounds of the surf breaking on the beach with their exquisite sensitivity to sound and vibration.

I imagine they are comfortable with the turbulence of chaos and change, that this is something I can learn in facing the innumerable thresholds of change in this life. The borders between water and earth are places where the spirits can enter. Turtles are the Keepers of the Doorways between the seen and the unseen.

Among all the sea turtles, leatherbacks are the strongest swimmers, especially fond of the open seas and deep water. They dive deeper than most whales. Only sperm whales and elephant seals dive deeper. They migrate thousands of miles every year, from icy Northern seas to the tropics. Coming into contact with people of many nations, leatherbacks remind us how connected we all are. Their habitat spans from the North Atlantic near the Arctic Circle to the South Pacific around New Zealand. Insulated by a fatty layer of tissue, leatherbacks can regulate their metabolism, almost like mammals, to avoid overheating or chilling. One additional sense they have is the ability to orient themselves to not only the grid but the intensity of the Earth's magnetic fields. They eat mainly jellyfish for sustenance. Jellyfish, which are 95% water, and look like light.

They do not lose their way.

As the oldest vertebrate animal in the world, a

symbol around the world of Mother Earth, the leatherback follows a songline of memory, appears as a blessing and a warning: Listen. Our future is at stake. In the Pacific Ocean, along the Mexico-Costa Rica shorelines, the population of leatherbacks has fallen 95% in just the last two decades. They have been on Earth twenty-five times longer than humans, but they could be gone forever in ten or fifteen years due to longline fishing, shrimp trawler nets, destruction by encroaching development of nesting sites, egg poaching, and the ubiquitous plastic debris which looks similar to the jellyfish they survive on.

During the three weeks I was in Costa Rica, the BP Deepwater Horizon oil well exploded in the Gulf of Mexico, primary home to the critically endangered green turtle called Kemps' Ridley. Their hatchlings are about to emerge and head for the sea. An oiled, poisonous sea. Young turtles are already being burned alive with desperate and ineffective attempts to contain the oil. Such short-term thinking, speed and greed, compared to the long life and wisdom of the turtle. It has not always been this way.

There was a time when Turtle had a starring role in many legends and creation myths of cultures and religions around the world. The ancient Maya imagined a circular earth as a great turtle afloat in a containing sea. In stories and myths from India, China, Japan, North America, she bears the weight of the world and has done so as Mother Earth for millions of years. The sea turtle was also sacred to Aphrodite, goddess of love and beauty.

In the Lakota creation story, there was another world before this one. But the people of that world did not behave themselves. Displeased, the Creative Power set out to make a new world. He sang several songs to bring rain, which poured stronger with each song. The earth split apart as water gushed up through the many cracks, causing a flood. By the time the rain stopped, all of the people and nearly all the animals had drowned. Only the turtle could dive deep enough and stay under long enough to retrieve a lump of mud from beneath the floodwaters. Singing, the Creating power shaped the mud and spread it on the water. He named the new land Turtle Continent and promised that all would be well if all living things learned to live in harmony. But the world would be destroyed again if they made it bad or ugly. We stand on Turtle Island. We have not learned to live in harmony. We are living in a turbulent time of transformation. What is our role in making the world well and whole again?

As a symbol of Mother Earth and the sacred

feminine, the leatherback has an urgent message for all of us. She carries millions of years of memory and magic. So do we, newcomers to this earth. Can we tune into our own deep wisdom, creativity, intuition?

Dive deep.

Take the long view.

Know we are all connected.

Offer your creativity extravagantly.

Persevere.

Open to mystery, trust your inner navigator.

Feast on light.

Become the world.

I returned from Costa Rica changed. My head quiet, my core humming. Certain that I could not figure out my future by thinking but would need to sink more deeply into blood wisdom, heart knowing. Awake to how we are all connected, continents by oceans, peoples by stories, and how the rhythms of nature are our own.

In surrender, my heart opened. Wiped out, I stepped into the void and found new ground. I have fallen in love with the new place.

My new home in California is a beautiful apartment on the water in Marin County, first seen in a meditation. I gather pictures of the leatherback for paintings, seeing in photographs her pink heated neck skin after laying her eggs, her blue-black back sprinkled with white dots like stars. Even the baby hatchlings are already strung with little pearls over their seven miniature ridges summoned by starlight. To paint these animals I buy larger canvases, the largest I have ever used.

"Let the drop of water that is you
become a hundred seas.
But do not think that the drop alone
becomes the ocean.
The ocean, too, becomes the drop."
- Rumi

Recommended Reading

Bohm, David. Wholeness and the Implicate Order (1980) London: Ark Paperbacks

Bolen, Jean Shinoda. Goddesses in Older Women: Archetypes in Women over Fifty (2002) Harper Perennial

- Urgent Message from Mother: Gather the Women, Save the World (2005) Conari Red Wheel

Capra, Fritjof. The Tao of Physics (1976) New York: Bantam

- The Web of Life: A New Scientific Understanding of Living Systems (1996) New York: Anchor

Coughlin, Linda; Ellen Wingard, and Keith Hollihan. (Eds.) Enlightened Power: How Women are Transforming the Practice of Leadership (2005) San Francisco: Jossey-Bass

Eisler, Riane. The Chalice and the Blade (1988) HarperOne

- The Real Wealth of Nations: Creating a Caring Economics (2008) Berrett-Koehler Publishers

Estes, Clarissa Pinkola. Women Who Run with the Wolves (1996) Ballantine Books

Gilligan, Carol. In a Different Voice: Psychological Theory and Women's Development (1993) 2d Edition Cambridge: Harvard University Press

Gimbutas, Marija. The Language of the Goddess (2001) Thames and Hudson

Griffin, Susan. Woman and Nature: The Roaring Inside Her (2000) 2d Edition Sierra Club Books

Helgesen, Sally. The Female Advantage: Women's Ways of Leadership (1995) Doubleday Currency

Hillman, James. The Myth of Analysis: Three Essays in Archetypal Psychology (1998) 3rd Edition Northwestern University Press

Houston, Jean. Jump Time: Shaping Your future in a World of Radical Change (2004) Sentient Publications

- with Mary Catherine Bateson. A Mythic Life: Learning to Live Our Greater Story (1996) HarperSanFrancisco

Jantsch, Erich. The Self-Organizing Universe (1980) Pergamon

Keller, Evelyn Fox. A Feeling for the Organism: The Life and Work of Barbara McClintock (1983) W.H. Freeman

Kristof, Nicholas and Sheryl WuDunn. Half the Sky: Turning Oppression into Opportunity for Women Worldwide (2010) Vintage Books

Lake, Orielle Osprey. Uprisings for the Earth: Reconnecting Culture with Nature (2010) White Cloud Press

Luke, Helen and Marion Woodman. The Way of Woman: Awakening the Perennial Feminine (1996) Image Books

Miller, Jean Baker. Toward a New Psychology of Women (1987) Beacon Press

Morrell, Rima A. The Sacred Power of Huna: Spirituality and Shamanism in Hawaii (2005) Inner Traditions

Moss, Robert. Dreaming the Soul Back Home: Shamanic Dreaming for Healing and Becoming Whole (2012) New World Library

Noble, Vicki. Shakti Woman: Feeling Our Fire, Healing Our World (1991) HarperSanFrancisco

Perera, Sylvia Brinton. Descent to the Goddess: A Way of Initiation for Women (1981) Inner City Books

Prigogine, Ilya. From Being to Becoming (1981) W. H. Freeman

- and Isabelle Stengers. Order Out of Chaos: Man's New Dialogue with Nature(1984) Shambhala

Shepherd, Linda Ph.D. Lifting the Veil: The Feminine Face of Science (1993) Shambhala

Stone, Merlin. When God Was a Woman (1978) Mariner Books

Tedlock, Barbara. The Woman in a Shaman's Body: Reclaiming the Feminine in Religion and Medicine (2005) Bantam Books

Wheatley, Margaret. Leadership and the New Science: Discovering Order in a Chaotic World (1999) Berrett-Koehler

Williams, Terry Tempest. Finding Beauty in a Broken World (2009) Vintage

Woodman, Marion. Addiction to Perfection (1982) Inner City Books
-Dancing in the Flames: The Dark Goddess in the Transformation of Consciousness (1997) Shambhala

About Marilyn Steele, Ph.D.

Marilyn Steele, Ph.D. is a Jungian psychologist, author, speaker, artist, and poet. She is a mother and grandmother. Marilyn practiced depth psychotherapy in Berkeley, CA for thirty years. Her work is dedicated to helping women access their wild feminine and returning feminine power to the world.

For more about Marilyn's work, please visit
www.thewildfeminine.com